This book, hopefully the first of many, is dedicated to Battersea,
in my veins for fifty years.

All Bible Quotations are from the New International Version, unless otherwise indicated.

All other quotations or references are indicated in the text.

In this book I repeatedly refer to three organisations:

The Providence House Trust *(www.providence-house) which has been my life for fifty years.*

The Shallowford Trust and East Shallowford Farm *(www.shallowfordfarm.co.uk) which has been a 'Lung for the City' for me and countless numbers of young people over many years.*

Waste not Want not Battersea *(www.wastenotwantnot-battersea.org) with whom I volunteered during Lockdown and beyond.*

Table of Contents

Introduction

Every day I write a blog, or almost every day. I call it Word for Today, not the most imaginative of phrases. It goes out by email each day to over seventy people, some of whom may not read it, or read it sometimes, and some read it each day without fail. It is also recorded and a further twenty- five receive it on their phones as an audio piece. I tweet it as an audio and post it also on Soundcloud. The MP has read it and so has the carpenter. The doctor has received it and so has the cook. The lawyer has read it and so has the electrician, so I must be doing something right.

As people do with these things, I write about what I see, and comment on what I hear or read. As to my seeing, it is often through the lens of being a community worker in Battersea. I have been based at Providence House, a youth and community centre in Falcon Road, just behind Clapham Junction station, for a year or two short of fifty years. What I write is coloured by that experience. Our work has an extension to a wonderful farm on Dartmoor, called East Shallowford, where for a few more years short of fifty, we have been taking young people and families for experiences to stretch the borders of their lives. I have mentioned that. In that locked down year of 2020, I had the opportunity to go out and about in the community with a project called Waste not Want not Battersea. That too gets a mention, as do one or two other things.

What I always write about is a thought from the Bible, because over many years it has been the lens through which I am able to see the world about me, the things that happen around us, and to understand and to encourage and to challenge us to better thinking. That is why it is a Word for Today.

I wrote many words in Lockdown, and this offering is a distillation of them: Words in a Lockdown Year. They have taken me through the streets of south London, navigating a pathway through this pandemic, reflecting on some of the bigger and smaller issues that have come up. Sometimes I write the narrative in the present and sometimes the past. Some of these words tell cameo stories of people in Lockdown. Some of these words give my take on things that have happened.

Always these words reflect faith. I trust too that always these words are readable.

Robert Musgrave MBE.

March 2021.

Providence House Trust

Chapter 1: God of this City

Lockdown Sunrise

I am in Battersea. In front of Providence House. It is 6 o'clock on a Sunday morning in April 2020. The sun has risen over Falcon Park, and is rising above the houses across the road. The sky is a clear grey.

It is quiet. I have seen one person walk by. Every minute or so a car passes. A 49 bus comes past along Falcon Road. Birds are singing. A magpie walks along the wall. A squirrel darts in among the rubbish on the street. A group of pigeons are having breakfast.

This is my city. This is our city. The song comes to my mind*:

"You're the God of this city. You're the King of these people. You're the Lord of this nation. You are...."

The corner shop will open today for papers and bits and pieces. The little supermarket has kept going all through this crisis, as has the butchers, and both will open this morning. Piggies cafe has shut down. Who knows whether they will rise again like the sun after this darkness! The barber's is closed but I have seen him around. The undertakers are busy, but not today. The Red Cross shop is shuttered down, but the clothes still pile up outside, and every few days we clear them up.

Who knows what will happen after lockdown is over? What businesses will still be there. What organisations will survive. Who will flourish.

That song again:

'You're the light in this darkness.
You're the hope to the hopeless.
You're the peace to the restless.
You are'

We've been here fifty years in this building. Sixty years in this community. Hundreds, thousands of young people, children, families have been through these solid blue doors. Hopefully doors that have represented hope. And hope is what is needed now. Hope for today. Hope for tomorrow. Hope for many tomorrows. Not just vague hope but God hope.

That song once more:

"There is no one like our God. There is no one like our God

For greater things have yet to come. And greater things are still to be done in this city."

We've sung that before. Do we believe it? Do I believe it? That there is more to be done here. That God has more to be done in this city, in this place, in this Providence.

"Greater things have yet to come. And greater things are still to be done in this city"

A prayer. From Psalm 68.

'Summon your power, O God. Show us your strength, O God, as you have done before.' Psalm 68.28.

'You are awesome, O God, in your place. You give power and strength to your people.' Psalm 68.35.

"You're the God of this city. You're the King of these people. You're the Lord of this nation. You are"

* Song: God of this City (Songwriters: Aaron Boyd / Andrew McCann / Ian Jordan / Peter Comfort / Peter Kernaghan / Richard Bleakley)

Finding a song

We were out and about in Battersea this week. I only go out once a week to help, and that is exhausting enough, but others go out every day. Somehow they can keep up the pace. I only really know what goes on in Battersea, but I suspect it is repeated all over the show. There are so many community champions. The champion I support is from Waste not Want not Battersea. It was late afternoon by the time I arrived. A local mum and her two daughters were sorting out food parcels. A local councillor and her daughter were going through boxes of French potatoes donated from somewhere. I just missed the MP, who had visited and joined the kitchen volunteers, chopping tomatoes. The volunteer chef is like a machine, never stopping, and there until the very end, when the shutter comes down, and she needs an uber to get her home, across London.

Out in the refrigerated van we went, down little side streets and pocket estates in Battersea, that I barely knew existed. Little communities, quietly shut up, but with a few people out and about, in the sunshine of this surreal springtime.

Frank no longer comes to the door of his terraced house but we talk with him through the window. We had pears for him this week. He was pleased about that. And can you believe it quails' eggs! Goodness knows where they came from! We stopped in the middle of the road to talk with the lady in the wheelchair by Union Grove to see if she needed anything. She took some potatoes and other bits. Peter has a terminal illness, confined indoors on the fourth floor, but on the phone, he exudes gratitude. You will never know how much all this has meant to me. He receives a couple of freshly cooked ready meals. We meet the lady with a young child on the street outside the courtyard of her flats near Plough Road. She brings a bag and fills it with things she knows how to cook. I stop and talk with a man I know, known him from boy to man, all my years at Providence. We talk. He tells me Seymour has succumbed to the virus. So that is two former Providence people I know of. Another former Providence person has been referred to Waste not Want not. He has a gaggle of small children to look after alone. He is grateful. Last week in the dark I trod on the little patch of earth in the little front yard. Mind the grass seeds he said. This week I was more careful. This week the grass is showing. A good sign for these days. By the time we got to Freedom Street it was saucepan banging time. Appropriate name for such a demonstration. Almost the whole street turned out to bang and clap. Another good sign for these days.

I was only the driver. That is an easy thing to do. There is a whole army of volunteers out there, coming together at a time like this, and others beavering away doing what they can, individuals with an idea, with a cause, with time to redeem.

During Covid-19, I have been making a slow passage through the book of Psalms. I have reached number 68. It includes these words, that combine gratitude with difficulty, and isolation with community, and trust:

'His name is the Lord – rejoice before him. A father to the fatherless, a defender of widows, is God in his holy dwelling. God sets the lonely in families, and leads forth the prisoners with singing.' Psalm 68.4-6.

I wasn't going to include the last phrase in the quotation, thinking it might not be pertinent. But it is. So many feel like prisoners at this time. The promise here is that God leads out the imprisoned, the confined, the isolated, with singing. This is a time for singing. This is a time when it is so important to find a song. The Psalmist found something to sing about in adversity. The Psalmist always found something to sing about. Something in his situation. Always something to sing about in God. This has never been so true.

Here is another line from Psalm 68, something to sing about:

'Praise be to the Lord, to God our Saviour, who daily bears our burdens. Our God is a God who saves – from the Sovereign Lord comes escape from death.'

It was 10.30 at night when I left Battersea towards my place of social isolation. Police cars were still whizzing up and down the roads, doubtless in pursuit of some breach, or worse. People were walking home. Cars travelling up and down the high road. The odd bus.

Psalm 68 ends simply. Appropriately. Praise be to God! A good way to end the day. A good way to start a new day.

The sound of singing has returned

"The manufacturer of food blenders has gone into liquidation, a dog kennel has had to call in the retrievers.

"The supplier of paper for origami enthusiasts has folded, the Heinz factory has been canned as they couldn't ketchup with orders.
"The tarmac laying company has reached the end of the road, the bread company has run out of dough.

"The specialist in submersibles has gone under, the bra manufacturer has gone bust, the clock manufacturer has had to wind down and gone cuckoo,

"The Chinese has been taken away, the shoe shop has had to put his foot down and given his staff the boot."

"And finally, the launderette has been taken to the cleaners."

All very amusing and clever, but the new look on the high road is without doubt the shutter. On Galpins Terrace, the Indian restaurant, the dry cleaner, shuttered. The post office, the bookie, Mr Shah's, shuttered. The law firm, the tattoo parlour, the travel shop, all shuttered. The DIY store has re-opened after being closed for several weeks. The gourmet burger, the jerk chicken, the chip shop all keep customers at a distance, and their windows are regaled with Covid-19 warning signs. The Tesco express has a respectful queue for fuel and provision customers alike.

The government has announced that there needs to be five things in place before lockdown can start to unlock. Will some of those shutters never clatter again as the chain is released, as the store opens for a new day? Will some of the workers having enjoyed working from home be reluctant to return to the office? Will the office prefer the cheaper option of not renting a premise, and business be a more remote enterprise? After all we have all got used to half of our lives being monitored or explained by a phone call via satellite to India. Maybe the remote will become the new near.

The church on Warwick Road is closed, but in its porch a light shines, with an appropriate message of prayer and hope. What will that look like when its doors finally open? Will the doors of some churches not finally open?

I want to make a promise. A spiritual promise. It is not about shutters or business. As I cannot make those. Nor is it about churches as such. It is about renewal. Spiritual renewal. The Bible throughout its pages promises hard times. We are in a hard time. It also promises renewal. Renewal and change and a renewed sense that God is present. It promises strength after weakness. Most of all love and closeness after distance.

I am not going to explain or comment on the next quotation from the Song of Songs. It is for you to understand it, both in terms of your own experience, and in your understanding of God and how He works.

'See! The winter is past. The rains are over and gone. Flowers appear on the earth and the season of singing has returned. The cooing of doves is heard again in our land. Arise, come, my darling, my beautiful one, come with me.' Song of Songs 2.11-13.

The numbers don't fit

There are lots of things today that don't quite seem to add up. We appear to get contradictory messages about what we can do, or what we will be able to do, or what will be advisable to do. In Switzerland they were saying hug the grandchildren. In the UK they were saying, whoa! Hold on, not so fast. We need more data. Data is of course a wonderfully mysterious word. Apparently we are desperate for it, depend on it for good judgement, never have enough of it.

Then there are the numbers. Numbers of cases and deaths. Numbers that tell only part of the story. Numbers that indicate a pattern. Criticism of the numbers that have been left out. Numbers as a target, which soon become numbers to judge and criticise politicians. Every day the government bulletin is about numbers. The numbers keep changing everyday.

There are other numbers. They are counted to measure good work. Numbers of volunteers, of food parcels delivered, of vulnerable people helped. Numbers – astonishing numbers sometimes – that tell of monies, given, promised, distributed, and probably held back too. And presented as a lifeline to keep a business or enterprise from going under, or possibly to postpone our reality checks.

I have my own numbers. They are of course quite small.

Now to change the focus slightly. I read Psalm 71. Whoever wrote it had a problem with numbers. For him at times it seemed life was filled with difficulties beyond his ability to count them. He was aware of evil in the world, though in this instance not of pandemic evil. 'Deliver me from the grasp of evil and cruel men.' He was aware of a world where false information could break out, contort life as a disease can do, such that he wanted to pray that 'his accusers would perish in shame'. He was worried about the loneliness of old age: 'Do not let me be cast away when I am old.'

He was worried too about the competing cries in his world between what was true and helpful, and what was made up, pernicious and designed to scare people, especially to scare him. In response he says: 'My tongue will tell of your righteous acts all day long.'

Now here is an interesting thing. Despite confessing that he had seen 'troubles many and bitter', he was curiously at peace about it all. He had come to that place in life, or rather that place in faith, where although he saw the many number of things in this world, in his time, that bewildered and besieged him, he increasingly saw, and felt, and experienced, the number of things that showed that God was good. That God was good to him. Always. In fact, he said that he couldn't get the numbers right. He couldn't make it all add up. Indeed it seemed to change each day.

This is what he said. Actually, this is what he sang:

'But as for me, I shall always have hope' – and that by the way is a pretty precious thing.

'But as for me, I shall always have hope. I will praise you, Lord, more and more.

'My mouth will tell of your righteousness, of your salvation all day long –

Even though I know not its measure.' Psalm 71.14-15.

There it is. He couldn't measure it. He couldn't count it. He couldn't get the numbers right. Too many, too much. The old English translation says – 'I know not the numbers thereof.'

These are the measurements that need to be important to us. These are the numbers we need to begin to look at, even though if we seriously, believingly look at them, we will soon lose the counting.

Despite perhaps confessing that we have seen 'troubles many and bitter', have we come to that place in faith, where although we see the many number of things in this world, in our time, that bewilder and besiege, we can increasingly see, and feel, and experience, the number of things that show that God is good. That God is good to us. That God is good to me.

'But as for me, I shall always have hope. I will tell of Your salvation all day long, though I do not know its measure.'

A good sign

There was a double rainbow over Battersea one night. It could be seen all over south London. It was seen in Surrey and Sussex too. A good sign.

I was out and about in Battersea again, following in the steps of the band of volunteers who work tirelessly for others. This is about more than food distribution. It is about people, contacting people, a word through a window, a meeting of the eyes, the opportunity to express gratitude, the opportunity for grace.

We haven't seen Frank now for three weeks, but he always speaks through the window. Last night we left some cheese outside. Another lady will only speak through her half open window, but says what she needs and a package is left. Jason has a sign on his door to say he prays for Boris. There is another one to pray for Donald and one for Jeremy. He tells us he has built a shed in his garden out of scrap wood during lockdown. He takes an armful of prepared meals. It took some weeks to get an answer from the lady on the corner, but now she knows the routine. I realise I knew her, and attended her husband's funeral last year, or was it the year before; and I helped her surviving son write his obituary. The old man down one of those hidden side streets along the Wandsworth Road is off on his constitutional walk, pushing with his walking support, shuffling forward. He doesn't really talk to us. Gruffs a bit. We leave food with the neighbour. She says she sorts him out and cooks a bit for him. I hadn't realised Wandsworth Road is a 20 mph zone. A camera flashes.

Round by Darlington House we give a lady some vegetables and plenty of carrots. Ironically over the high brick wall is New Covent Garden market, and at 5am Waste Not Want Not collected surplus supplies from market traders. It took around 15 hours then to get them to this second floor house. Might have been quicker to lob them over the wall! Three young men were greasy hands under the bonnet of a car. Not sure they knew what they were doing. We reversed the van carefully out of the narrow street.

We were in Tennyson Street when the eight o'clock clapping started. This is another good sign. We drove slowly down the road tooting the horn. It was Tennyson who wrote: "Pray for my soul. More things are wrought by prayer than this world dreams of: Wherefore, let thy voice, rise like a fountain for me night and day." Perhaps that is another sign. Prayer.

By the time we reached Winstanley Estate it was dark, raining dropping damp from the plane trees, the last of the bird song until another day. The square was empty. The rain had washed away the men who stand there most of the day, socially distant, talking, smoking, perhaps waiting until this is all over. Not so tonight.

Jesus spoke about the weather. Maybe weather a bit like we had yesterday. I think he was a bit fed up with the pontifications of people who liked to say a lot, when in reality they said very little. Or very little of importance. These people asked Jesus for a sign from heaven. He replied, probably with one of those characteristic Jesus sighs, that these people were good at making predictions about the weather. It looks like rain tomorrow. I think it will be a good day for ploughing. Red sky at night, shepherds delight. And so on. Then he fixed his gaze on them and said clearly 'but you cannot interpret the signs of the times.' How we need that today! To interpret the signs of the times. For leaders to speak with clear thought, clear leadership, clear counsel, and with humble recognition and serious faith.

Anyway to his audience, Jesus left a riddle: to a generation that only looks for the sensational and short-lived, the only sign you will get will be 'the sign of Jonah'. Jesus then left them and went away. (Matthew 16.1-4). Jonah? Why is he talking about Jonah? You can still imagine the questioning in their voices. The sign of Jonah, three days in the belly of a great fish, was a clear signpost to Jesus death and burial and rising from death on the third day. Now that was a sign. That is a sign.

The apostle Paul in his letter to the Romans in the New Testament wrote, that Jesus 'was declared to be the Son of God, by his resurrection from the dead: Jesus Christ our Lord.' Romans 1.4. Truth is that is a sign for every generation. It is a sign for every believing, trusting person. It is a sign for every seeking, looking person. It is a sign for everyone who looks at the world and asks why. It is my sign. It should be all our signs: that Jesus Christ is Lord. It changes our perspective on life. On death. On these times. On all times.

It was the first of May. That was another sign. A sign of spring. But look for that greater sign.

Chapter 2: C is for Community

Prayer for my city

I got up one morning in May around dawn. Probably foolishly. I got in the car in Norbury and drove along the high road. The shops were silent. There were few cars on the road.

They call this high road, Streatham High Road, the longest high street in Europe. I suppose it is, beginning in the south with Croydon and running all the way along past Brixton with barely a bend in the road. Three people at the bus stop, yards apart. Someone waiting at most bus stops. As I drove under the railway bridge a train passed on its way to central London.

Streatham Common was quiet with cars filling at the petrol station. The statue of the soldier stood sentinel on the corner, a reminder of so many men and women, lost to this city in wars. Now we are counting the cost of men and women lost to a silent, but equally deadly viral warfare.

The mega Tesco store was closed, but patiently waiting to open its great glass doors later in the morning. A man on a bike, past the one shop open on the entire high road, Bells the newsagent. Buses up and down the high road, linking south Londoners with all parts of town – Old Coulsdon, Croydon, Kingston, South Kensington, Euston.

There were no signs of activity at the bottom of the hill below St

Leonards where the north African community trade and gather. Everything is still shuttered. Manna Christian Centre is shut of course. No Bibles have been sold there for a while.

Past the old Police Station, the street cleaner was at work. A police patrol car passed the place where the terrorist was shot not many months ago – who remembers that now. Passed where Pratts department store used to be – who remembers that now. Passed where banks are now coffee shops, but where coffee shops have had to be closed to ironically keep people out, because social mixing has become a social contagion.

Down Sternhold Avenue a jogger crosses the road, and turning into Telford, I stopped outside the church, St Thomas's. This church built over a hundred years ago, because so many homes were being built in Telford Park, but without a place of worship nearby. Built really as a mission outreach church from neighbouring St Leonard's. Built because men and women, boys and girls, of this our city needed to hear the good news that Jesus Christ saves, needed a place to gather where they could give praise to God for all his gifts, needed a place where they could turn aside from the concerns of this passing world and turn their attention to something eternal, someone eternal, the only wise God and Saviour, Father, Son and Holy Spirit. They needed a place of prayer, a place to pray for themselves, to pray for their city.

This morning I stood outside our empty church. The bells no longer ring. The doors are barred shut. They are barred all over the country. I went and sat on the bench, among the scent of the garden, looking out past the ash trees, and asked myself when we could do all that again in this place. Would it be the same? Could it be the same? How would it be the same?

Certainly the same in this one sense – Jesus Christ, the same, yesterday, today, forever.

Certainly this doesn't change either: 'The dawn leads on another day. The voice of prayer is never silent, nor dies the strain of praise away.' John Ellerton.

This, too, remains the same: 'Rejoice always, pray without ceasing, give thanks in all circumstances; for this is the will of God in Christ Jesus for you.' 1 Thessalonians 5.

C is for Community

C is for community. I am sure not if you played an alphabet game what your ABC would be. One week in the spring Lockdown the Providence House and friends YES project produced a video of the song 'We are Family', which featured various people with shots to show A is for Art, etc. If you get the chance to see it, it is well worth your while. In my ABC, I think my C would always be C is for Community.

At present in the current restrictions, Thursday is my out and about in Battersea, out and about in the Community, day. A bit around Providence House and then my weekly volunteer driver shift. It is always about people, so it is always about Community. It's a bit obvious really, but Community is all about people, all about connections. All about colour – the colourfulness of character and interactions and people's lives.

C is for Community. Talking with the next door landlord, a talkative Irishman, about the leaking pipe from the shop empty during Covid, and what do we do. The man with the Liverpool accent who patiently hoses the planted area behind Providence and smiles at passers-by. The boy with enquiring eyes, accompanied by his tutor, eyes sparkling with questions. At 4pm I get in the car to go to the other end of Battersea. (Apparently about 20 minutes later there is an incident across the road from Providence, with a worried man carrying a machete worrying everyone. Police deal with it.)

C is for Community. The volunteers at the centre finishing after the long day. Three furloughed women who work without ceasing preparing food. Three smiling young men who meet the public and hand out the food parcels. The chef from a London museum, closed for Covid, but day by day cooking for people, cooking for the project.

C is for Community. The Spanish speaking lady, who spoke for ages on the phone, all anxiety, all apology, comes out of her house with a baby, grateful, thankful for the food parcels. Frank is out down his street, not talking through the window today. He takes cheese and butter and some meals. The man further up the road, who doesn't usually come to the door, chats. He is elderly, disabled, and he tells of his experience with Covid-19, the coldness and the fever, intermixed with the fear. Now he smiles. (It was around 4.30 when we drove past the junction of Queenstown and Wandsworth Road, and people were patiently queuing outside Sainsburys. When we came past the junction around 7pm, police were all over the area, both sides of the road cordoned off. The dread of uncertainty).

C is for Community. We drop some food to a lady referred to us on an estate. In the street two lads we know are fixing a moped, shiny tools all over the path, hands full of grease, cold hands in the cold wind. One of them seems to know what he is doing. By some flats on York Road Estate, an Ethiopian family stop to talk, and take some butter and cheese. Lots of butter and cheese today. On Surrey Lane, at the entrance to a tower block, someone leaves each day a tray of artisan bread, which people come and take. A resident has pinned to the wall a lovely thank you note to the anonymous supplier. We drive down Lombard Road around 9pm. If we had come the day before we might have witnessed the knife attack on two young men, a car chase, ambulances and police, all reported in the media. We have worked with one of the young men, and have since heard he is ok.

C is for Community. Near Battersea High Street, we stopped to looked at a so-called art installation. I cannot really describe it, but it is behind some railings, on a patch of grass, outside a ground floor window. We know the person, and the more we know him the more we realise that he is unusual. He comes out and shows the art work off. Three large onions impaled on the iron railings. A box of vegetables, various lengths of cloth. A tray of what looks like a Mediterranean tea apparatus. Various slogans, and a hand written message to the jobsworth from the council who has written to tell him to dismantle it all. He climbs in through his open window, because he appears to have boarded up his front door. He never stops talking. C is for Community.

Community is about open doors and closed doors. It is about talking and silence. It is about engagement and privacy. It is about people. If I was brave enough, or faithful enough, or serious enough, I would have this as my vision for community. It is from the prophet Zechariah in the Old Testament who lived at a time when his people were seeking to re-build community, physically, socially, spiritually. I have adapted the words.

'Where community is a place and home for all people, where men and women, and those of ripe old age will take part, where the streets will be filled with boys and girls playing and learning, and young people discovering, exploring, finding who they are, where people of different languages, cultural and social background will come in and say, 'Let us go with you, because we have heard that God is with you'. Where community will be known as a place of welcome, of truth and as God's House.'

This is the Word of the Lord (Adapted from Zechariah 8).

Twenty-Two Yards

Twenty-two yards is socially distant enough. Probably fifteen or maybe ten at the point of delivery. Left knee raised, left arm pointing towards the wicket. Whirl of arms and legs, flight of red, bounce. Forward press, left elbow raised, crack! Sound of leather on willow, bat on ball, red bouncing towards extra cover. Back in the nets on the Common after eight weeks or more. The council removed the steel barriers to open this facility up again. Good to be back.

The parakeets still screech howzat as they fly from tree to tree. The blackthorn and hawthorn have both blossomed in the meantime, and now their dark green leaves create the backdrop to this little scene. Traffic rumbles along the South Circular, but without the queues of previous months. The wail of a siren, the guttural rev of a motor bike.

By the pond the all-night take-away still serves coffee and bacon rolls. I wonder if it is all night in these times. The waterfowl are oblivious to the changes. Coots, moorhens, mallards, Muscovy ducks. Geese cruising maternally with a trail of goslings in their wake. Twenty-five we counted another day. The heron. The cormorants. Now the other fishermen are back also, exercising their recovered rights with line and tackle patiently by the side.

It is good to be back in the nets. The apostle Paul made an obvious statement in writing to a man, much younger than me: 'Physical exercise is good.' Perhaps he was saying to Timothy that he should get out more. It is good advice. I guess in this day it needs to also be careful advice. I spoke with a former Wandworth councillor, she being over seventy, and she still has felt the time is not yet right to venture out. At least she has a garden.

The apostle Paul went onto qualify his statement about exercise. Perhaps it was the opposite to what I said, and he was saying to Timothy that he should get out less: 'Physical exercise has some value in it, but spiritual exercise is valuable in every way, for it promises life both for now and for the future.' 1 Timothy 4.8.

Either way the apostle is emphasising personal engagement with God as the best training in life. He writes a similar thing to Timothy in a second letter, and this is good advice for us to:

'But as for you, continue in what you have learned and have become convinced of, and how from infancy you have known the scriptures, which are able to make you wise for salvation through faith in Christ Jesus.

'All scripture is God-breathed and is useful for teaching, rebuking, correcting and training in righteousness, so that the man or woman of God may be thoroughly equipped for every good work.' 2 Timothy 3.15-17.

So get out your walking shoes or your running shoes, or get out when and where you can; but please, do not forget that deeper exercise – the Word of God, the Word of God and you.

Best exercise. Best training.

Driving straight

Out and about in Battersea dropping food and meals off, working with Waste not Want not. There seems to have been a shift in the needs. In some ways it may not be so necessary to keep the deliveries going each week. In some ways it might remain critical. Either way, I will probably we doing it less as July shifts gear into August.

This then is one for the road.

Elena from Estonia is loading the van. We stop at the restaurant where Carmela is Italian and is helping her brother. Betty from Ethiopia helps carry things from the van.

In the street we meet Leslie from the Library, who talks through her mask, and Ade from the airport who works in security. Emma from Addlestone is passing and stops and tells us about the community café she helps run in the church. Debra from the Red Cross has locked up shop and is going home, and Joanna the nurse stays for a long chat.

Thomas's trousers are falling down but he is wearing two pairs. He sorts himself out and then approaches another pedestrian for money. The red-faced man is always polite when we see him, but looks a bit thinner or slimmer since I last saw him. He is living in a hotel but comes out each day to beg near the station. He comes from Romania, and so do the voluble working men who meet up and talk and drink by the bench under the plane tree.

On the road we stop by Belinda from Belize, who has the small child and is always appreciative. There had been a call from Asher from Ashley Crescent, and so we park the van there and fill some bags with good things. A lady calls me from the third floor window. She always calls me 'farda'. It is a bit like calling me 'uncle'. She is a former Providence member who keeps in regular touch. This is where she now lives.

Genar from the ground floor on Whitnell Way is always glad to see the van arrive, but always has to be told to keep his distance. Harry from up the hill is also visited. He wants to know if we have a fridge freezer as his has packed in. We don't forget Sam from Surrey Lane, bringing up three kids on his own, two of whom peer behind his legs to see what's going on. Minnie from Minshull Street is more than grateful. She wants to hug, which is not a good idea. She is in poor health. The block of flats appears to be in poor health. The ground floor flats are all boarded up with steel cages. The rest look like they are waiting for the same, but meanwhile fifty or so families live upstairs in the brown brick flats without a lift.

The last call is to the most appreciative of couples. They talk about angels and wings and gladly accept the food. We park the van on another housing estate. I am done for this week, although the project of course goes on.

What also goes on is Community. Remember C is for Community.

Chapter 3: Only one place to go

Sunrise Easter Sunday

It is 6.15 in the morning and I am on Pollards Hill, 200 feet above sea level. A fox turns from scrabbling in the grass to look at me. The sounds of morning are just beginning and there is a glow of dawn across the distant hills. Below me and all around is south London. This is my town. At least my part of town. It is your town too. It is any town in any country. It is any town in the world.

Towards the south I can see the twin towers of former industry and present commerce, IKEA, and the Purley Way. Rising out of the near distance is the town centre with its tower blocks for business and local government and high-rise dwellings, full of people, hemmed in, waiting for the dawning of another day. Below me and around me are the lines of roof tops, and streets and houses and trees between, each with their own story of culture and belief, of troubles and joys, and all about to face what today will bring to each.

Towards the east, where the first light of morning comes, that tall icon of communication, the mast on Crystal Palace, symbol of every WhatsApp and Zoom, and television and satellite phone. Somewhere below it, I can just see the grey spire, of which church I cannot work out, but still pointing heavenwards, whose bells will ring out today from an empty church – that Christ is Risen. He is risen indeed. The empty church almost empty like the tomb. But Christ is not tomb bound or church bound. Christ is risen. He is risen indeed.

The birds are in full song now. The shadows on the distant hills are lightening. The streaks of grey and yellow, of changing light. Now it begins. It begins to creep above the horizon. Golden orb. The light of morning. The light of day. The beginning of something new.

The one place to go

We are running out of places to go. The theatres and cinemas are closed. The restaurants are closed, but if you are lucky, and you need it, there may be some takeaways you can access, if you do so carefully. The churches are closed. I was told this is the first time they have been closed wholesale for over 700 years. Hitler couldn't close our churches, but Covid has. Even the parks are getting closed. I thought we were doing something sensible by going to Richmond Park on the Saturday before it all started, as after all, if you can keep a social distance anywhere, surely there. It was difficult. It was hugely busy. I know a man who has left home, bought a camper van and now lives in his daughter's driveway, communicating by paper messages through the letter box. We are running out of places to go.

In a different context, long ago, and different times, Moses thought about this question. He deals with it in Deuteronomy chapter 19. He was worried in this instance not about the spread of disease, but the spread of anger. In a time where community infrastructure was weak and barely set up, how do you manage angry people who want to carry out their own justice, without waiting for the law to get involved. What happens, for instance, if me and a colleague are working and a fatal accident happens, and I get the blame. Honest, it was an accident! Where can I go, before angry relatives come for me? Moses said to set up a number of cities throughout the land, where such a person can run to for safety. They are called in the Bible, Cities of Refuge. They became a place, where if a man got there in time, he could self-isolate. Not self-isolate from disease, though Moses did have ideas for that also, but self-isolate from angry, predatory men. Trouble with this is that although it might have saved a person's life, it may well have broken up his family.

So back to the earlier statement: we are running out of places to go. Please don't skim over this next statement. There is one place we can always go. I am not presenting an alternative to social distancing, or self-isolating, because you have to do that. It is your sensible and practical and Christian response to this expansive pandemic. There is one place we can always go. It is for inner safety. It is for inner safety when all around nowhere is safe. It is a place to go, when other places we cannot go. It is to Jesus. This we must take seriously, practically, spiritually.

Charles Wesley wrote these words in one of his songs: "Other refuge have I none, hangs my helpless soul on You. Leave, oh, leave me not alone, still support and comfort me.

"All my trust on You is stayed, all my help from You I bring. Cover my defenceless head with the shadow of your wing."

Every word of this song needs thinking about. Every word here needs praying through. To be truthful, it is a song for those oppressed through Covid 19. It is also a song for those oppressed by all of life's unmeaning. It is especially a song for those awakened to that deeper, more deadly virus within the human heart, my own sin, my own disregard of God and His grace. It is a song for those running out of places to go. Christ is the City of Refuge.

"Jesus, lover of my soul, let me to Your bosom fly, while the nearer waters roll, while the tempest still is high. Hide me, O my Saviour, hide, till the storm of life is past. Safe into the haven guide.

O receive my soul at last."

Busy hands, busy minds, busy hearts

There was a mild frost again on this April spring morning. Let's hope the frost is only on the ground and not in our hearts. The blossom on the cherry is still shining white in the morning sun. Behind the blossom the leaves are pushing out and the blossom will soon fall like snow in the breeze. It is a good sign. Things are moving on. Nature is not on hold, even if some of our lives seem to be.

Four hundred thousand have volunteered to support the NHS. Our doctor friend is working in A&E for the next three weeks; she asks for prayer, because it will be very challenging.

I watched Paul the taxi driver post a note through the letter box of the elderly man with mobility issues, to offer help. On our daily walk we passed a lady sat in her front garden, self-isolating, but not closed off from the world. I passed a woman on the phone, crying and screaming to someone and complaining of those in her life she can no longer trust and disavowing that her life still had any purpose.

Mr Shah's shop is shuttered up. The petrol station is closed. The pharmacist is open for set hours with a sign about access. Pete is working on a building site in Devon and says there is nothing to come back for to London. He will try and find work down there. He sent this verse to me, from Isaiah 26.20, but I'm not sure if it was to worry me or encourage patience: 'Go, my people, enter your rooms and shut the doors behind you. Hide yourselves for a little while, until His wrath is passed.'

People are talking with each other in new ways. There is a rise in altruism. Pray God that there will not be a rise in the opposite. Moses, in Deuteronomy chapter 22, says that in good times or hard times, we should always look out for our neighbour. 'If you see your brother's ox or sheep straying, do not ignore it but be sure to give it back to him. Do the same if you find your brother's donkey or his coat or anything he loses. Do not ignore it.' In other words, look out for others. Phone someone you haven't been in contact with today. Message another. Get in touch with those you are out of touch with.

Busy hands, busy minds, busy hearts.

At this time God is looking for something transformative in the way we act: 'Each of you should look not only to your own interests but also to the interests of others.' At this time God is looking for something transformative in the way we think: 'Do nothing out of selfish ambition or vain conceit, but in humility consider others better than yourselves.' At this time God is looking for something transformative in the way we feel: 'Your attitude should be the same as that of Christ Jesus, who, being in very nature God, did not consider equality with God something to be grasped, but made himself nothing, taking the very nature of a servant.' Philippians2.3-4.

Busy hands, busy minds, busy hearts.

God on the move

It is 7am. The workman from the house across the road has come out to face the morning. They are all builders in this house of multi-occupancy, part of the army of overseas workers who service our construction industry. He is short, stocky going on portly, but I suspect his hands and arms lift many a heavy weight each day. He is dressed for work. The first thing he does is look up at the sky and stare. The second thing he does is slowly cross himself. Maybe that is his prayer for the day. Maybe that is his plea to God for protection as he goes out into what is for many a hostile environment. Thirdly he puts his brown cloth cap on and waits for his lift to work – the maroon Vauxhall saloon that arrives on time every morning. Cloth cap gets in with two housemates. Best of luck!

Perhaps there is a wing and prayer about the way we handle the whole thing, a hoping for the best mixed with the application of science; because as they keep repeating, this is an unprecedented time. The government has, of course, issued a stream of guidelines and rules, for the most part being kept, and as they plot their course, with a mixture of judgment and guesswork, they in turn get frustrated by the ignorance or defiance displayed by members of the public; witness the story of a friend whose passage along a pavement was blocked by removal men, laughing at the idea of social distancing.

During Lent in Lockdown, I doggedly kept to a course of producing a Word for the Day, that referenced a section each day from the book of Deuteronomy in the Bible, as a daily reflection, following the broad theme of 'the Pilgrim's Way'. During Lockdown it seemed to be viewed through the lens of the pandemic. This chapter holds extracts from those daily offerings.

Without doubt Deuteronomy is about a different age altogether, and about issues that broadly we might find irrelevant or even distasteful to modern eyes. However, like us Moses was trying to make sense of how people should live in community, live in their world, live within the challenges of their day, and not descend into chaos; but rather persist in principles of godliness and fairness, and of preserving faith and truth. Not too different in essence then from government today. How do we give the best advice, how do we back up the advice with constraint if it is ignored, do we suspend freedoms because the health needs of the nation are of more importance? Interesting times, troubling times.

Where in all this is the path for the man or woman with faith, or are they too reduced to a wing and a prayer plus a dose of self-isolation? Is all they have a glance up at the morning sky, making the sign of the cross and putting on the cloth cap?

I have found in Deuteronomy chapter 23 a nugget of encouragement. 'The Lord your God moves about in your camp to protect you and to deliver your enemies to you.' (verse 14). As a spiritual principle it shines out like the morning sun, even if the sentences around it would take some unpicking. Translate it to your life, to your movements, to your faith community, and think this, that God is moving about to protect you. In different expressions, this theme runs throughout the Scripture, that God is with those who trust, who look to Him for help, who come to Him through the Lord Jesus, who did far more than 'move around the camp.'

Yes, I will look up the sky, but I will do it, echoing the thought of that great Psalm: 'I will lift up my eyes to the hills – to the skies. I will ask myself the question – where does my help come from? (Is it a wing and a prayer, a hope for the best?)

'My help comes from the Lord, the Maker of heaven and earth, who will not let your foot slip, who will watch over your coming and going, both now and forevermore.' Psalm 121.

Song for Sunday

Sundays are for singing. It was always so. God made it so.

At the weekend we took our permitted daily exercise, and walked through Mitcham Common. A robin sang solo, red throat throbbing with pure sound, high among the white blossom of a tree. He sang alone, but sang for everyone. Three crows squabbled and croaked in a hawthorn tree. A pair of tits darted among a thicket of scrub, chasing each other for love. A blackbird, with that most princely voice in all the wood, sang his full range of notes. He sang it for today. He will sing it again for Sunday. Above it all, silent, watchful, the kestrel hovered and glided, reddish plumage glinting in the sun.

Sundays are for singing. It was always so. God made it so.

Moses had a song. I expect he had a fine voice that could project its range across the hills of Moab. In the book of Psalms there is one song attributed to him, Psalm 90. Not surprisingly it is about our mortality, how we live our lives in the light of God, trouble and sorrow, joy and gladness. 'Number our days aright', he sings, 'that we may gain a heart of wisdom.' As you would also expect from Moses, he sings about God, his God, and frames our short life in the picture of God's eternity: 'Lord, you have been our dwelling place throughout all generations. Before the mountains were born or you brought forth the earth and the world, from everlasting to everlasting you are God.'

Moses also has a song in Deuteronomy chapter 32. Almost as if to say, enough of talking, now for some singing. He sings a story, of God's good grace, of his people being the apple of his eye. It is also a story of regret and failure, of breach of trust between man and God. It is a song of judgment and of mercy. It is a song of God and his ways: 'O praise the name of our God. He is the Rock, his works are perfect, and all his ways are just. A faithful God who does no wrong, upright and just is he.' A good song, I would say, for a Sunday.

But there is another song that Moses sang. Literally his swansong. It is found in chapter 33. It is like the father of the nation speaking to his people, a bit like the Queen has done during Covid-19. He takes each of the tribal families in turn, and sings something prophetic to each. Sometimes it is a warning from the past, or warning from the future. Sometimes it is a promise from yesterday, or a promise to come. For the tribe of Asher, the people group you have probably least heard of from the children of Israel, he says these eternal words. These are indeed a song for Sundays. A song for every Sunday:

'There is no-one like our God, who rides on the heavens to help you and on the clouds in his majesty.

The eternal God is your refuge, and underneath are the everlasting arms.' Deuteronomy 33.26-27.

Now there is a song for Sundays, and for weekdays: underneath are the everlasting arms. There is a song for lockdown and after lockdown.

Chapter 4: Pandemic of Grace

Pandemic of Racism

One Sunday afternoon in late May, I was sent a music video. There were two rappers, or perhaps they were grime artists. One of them I have known since he was a boy. He is black of African parentage, but born and bred in Battersea. Now he is well over six foot, muscles bulging out of his chest and arms. The last time I saw him just before lockdown was at a celebration for a lad lost to violence some years before. The music video is set against a background of Lavender Hill and Clapham Junction, with Arding and Hobbs in the background. There are two singers parading their stuff in front of a crowd of young black men each clad in a black tee shirt with 'Warrior' on it, and with various placards being held.

I guess it's a protest song. It's about black oppression, suppression, survival and revival 'Lost my brother to the street, lost my brother to police, lost my brother to the system.' 'There's a war going on outside. You can look deep in the eyes and see the distrust. Just a verbal picture you could cut and paint with a brush.' It all fits the current mood.

So they pulled old Edward Colston off his plinth and now he has sunk to the bottom of the harbour, where doubtless his slave ships docked all those bleak years ago. Mayor Marvin Rees, himself a symbol of the fusion a mixed society can be, said he should have come down long ago. "People in Bristol who don't want that statue in the middle of the city came together and it is my job to unite, hear those voices and hold those truths together for people for whom that statue is a personal affront."

The two archbishops of the Church of England issued a joint statement to be read in churches, appropriate I suppose to show the black and white faces of the national church in the hope that this was some kind of message of unity. The church has clearly got something right at the top, at least until the following week, when Archbishop John retired; even if it doesn't always trickle down to all the parish pews. The statement read that "Systemic racism continues to cause incalculable harm across the world. Our hearts weep for the suffering caused – for those who have lost their lives, those who have experienced persecution, those who live in fear. Let us be clear: racism is an affront to God. It is born out of ignorance, and must be eradicated."

As Dr Martin Luther King Jr said, and I doubt any of us can deny it: "In a real sense, we are all caught in an inescapable network of mutuality, tied in a single garment of destiny. Therefore, injustice anywhere is a threat to justice everywhere."

The Home Secretary and the Prime Minister took to the microphone. They have tried to get a message to both the audiences that might be listening, that Black Lives Matter, but so does Law and Order. Maybe you can touch old Colston, but keep your hands off Churchill.

On Sunday a fox came into our garden with her cub. Don't understand why she can't read the notices to keep out. Usually when a fox comes along, I look to see if the cat is alright and then I tell him or her to shove off. Not in my back yard! This time we were intrigued and watched them roll around a bit on the grass, before not outstaying their welcome. Maybe there is some sort of parable here. Were they welcome or were they not? In many ways it is a confusing world and not just for foxes. But then perhaps it isn't and things really are black and white, and clear and straightforward. Or as Luther King said, 'we are all caught in an inescapable network of mutuality.'

This is a Word for the Day, so I want to bring in a Bible reference, a thought to carry through the day, but I don't want to throw up some neat platitude, to tick someone's box and feel okay. There is a passage in Acts chapter 13, a three sentence snapshot of a Christian community, a bit of a diverse community that had come together strongly. The simple narrative is that there were a group of praying leaders in the city of Antioch, now in modern day Syria, who regularly met together, and on one occasion God by the Holy Spirit speaks to them as a group and says that two of them have been chosen to spread the good news about Jesus. It is significant because it marks the beginning of the spread of Christianity from Jewish migrant backwaters across Europe and then eventually across the world to all nations, and ultimately to you and me.

They were certainly a mixed bunch, forged into a band of brothers, by God's 'inescapable network of mutuality'. Paul or Saul of Tarsus, born and bred a bigot, who until Christ changed him, hated with a greater passion than a man can love. Manaen whose upbringing was among the ruling and political classes. Barnabas everyone's favourite uncle, who was given the nickname 'son of encouragement'. Lucius of Cyrene, with a Roman name but a north African passport, if they had ID cards in those days. And Simeon the Niger, or Simeon the black. I doubt that his nickname was because he wore black tee-shirts. Another thing: he wasn't there to make up the numbers, to fill up some racial quota, to the tick the equality box for the bishop's inspection. He was there because he was one of the brothers, a man of faith, part of the network of mutuality. He was there, as the others were, because the Holy Spirit had brought them together. He had forged such a unity.

Here was a real unity, a genuine anti-racism, a working inclusion. These people prayed together. They fasted together. They heard God speak together. They heard the Holy Spirit give instructions together. They laid hands on Paul and Barnabas and commissioned them – together. There was a God inspired, God knit network of mutuality. Brought together by spiritual power and not political legislation.

Here is a truth: The Holy Spirit is at the heart of genuine Christian unity.

Here is another truth from Paul's Letter to the Ephesians (4.2-6) in the Bible: 'Be completely humble and gentle. Be patient, bearing with one another in love. Make every effort to keep the unity of the Spirit in the bond of peace. There is one body and one Spirit – just as you were called to one hope when you were called – one Lord, one faith, one baptism, one God and Father of all, who is over all and through all and in all.'

By the way the fox came into the garden again. For a short while. Then he or she casually sloped away beside the garden shed.

Pandemic of Inequality

There is another pandemic. A pandemic of inequality, or perhaps it is better expressed as a pandemic of injustice. The other pandemics feed off it, and the effect of the pandemic of coronavirus, or for that matter the pandemic of racism, hurts the poor more disproportionately than where there is a bit of wealth.

The newsfeeds have been all over it. The lockdown is hurting the education of the poor disproportionately. It will do the same in the economic recession and search for work. It will have its effect in health care. If only it gets reported, it will be shown to hit hardest in certain communities throughout the world. There is going to be a lot hurting. It might be said that it was ever thus. That is not the point. As David Shepherd, when Bishop of Liverpool wrote in 1983, in his book 'Bias to the Poor', "The burden of unemployment and disadvantage falls unequally on our divided society. It hits the urban poor most sharply. These people are robbed of choices which God wills for all human beings. The Gospel is both about changing people from inside out and changing the course of events to set people free."

The Bible has a lot to say about injustice and justice. It says that justice is central to who God is. 'Righteousness and justice are the foundation of Your throne, O God. Love and faithfulness go before you.' Psalm 89.14. The Bible shows that God has a bias to the poor. Our world, our society, and probably our lives, show a bias against the poor.

Isaiah the prophet ridiculed the hollowness and hypocrisy of the form of religion without the heart, and firmly said that God doesn't like it: 'On the day of your fasting (and religious celebrations) you do what suits you, and exploit your workers. Your ceremonies end in quarrelling and strife and in striking each other with wicked fists. This is the kind of religion I have chosen, says the Lord: to loose the chains of injustice and untie the cords of the yoke. To share your food with the hungry and to provide the poor wanderer with shelter; and when you see the naked to clothe him, and not to turn away from your own flesh and blood.' Isaiah 58.

Jesus said at the beginning of his ministry, very deliberately, very consciously, and at a particularly chosen location, the synagogue in his home town: 'The Spirit of the Lord is upon me, because he has anointed me to preach good news to the poor. He has sent me to proclaim freedom for the prisoners and recovery of sight for the blind, to release the oppressed, to proclaim the day of the Lord's favour.' Luke 4.14-18. Jesus had a bias to the poor, and not everybody liked it.

There is another pandemic that has broken out. A pandemic of blame, a fever of exposing the past, some of which may undoubtably be a good thing. The exposure of men on a pedestal who gave with the one hand, but took away far more with the other. Some of this resonates with words that Jesus spoke: 'There is nothing concealed that will not be disclosed, or hidden that will not be made known. What you have said in the dark will be heard in the daylight, what you have whispered in the ear in the inner room will be proclaimed from the rooftops.' Luke 12.2-3. It almost literally echoes the words of the apostle Paul: 'So if you think you are standing firm, be careful that you don't fall.' 2 Corinthians 10.12.

Paul, of course, wasn't talking about the high and mighty. He was talking about the everyday person. Speaking of which, we spend a lot of time making it all about them and what they have done and little time about what we have done or rather failed to do. The apostle John, in his letter in the Bible added his bit: 'If anyone has material possessions and see his brother in need but has no pity on him, how can the love of God be in him. Dear children, let us not love with words or tongue, but with actions and in truth.' 1 John 3.17-18.

Jesus told a story of a rich man and a poor man, Lazarus, who daily hung around the rich man's gate. And never once did the rich man lift a finger to help, and even the dogs in the house were better off than Lazarus, feeding off the scraps from the dinner table. The story then goes on to talk about heaven and hell and regrets that cannot be reversed. It is a fine thing to talk about injustice, but trust me, we all have a Lazarus at our doors, or in our lives, or even in our families, who we pay scant attention to. Maybe we should coin a phrase that justice begins at home. Or even injustice begins at home.

There is indeed a pandemic of injustice. Unfortunately, the pandemic of injustice has caught us all. It is no respecter of persons. It crosses racial barriers, class barriers, economic barriers, faith barriers. You don't need a thermometer to check whether you have it. Just look out for Lazarus outside your door, or at work, or in your family, next time you think of ignoring them, or unthinkingly walk past.

'O Lord, who may dwell in your sanctuary? Who may live on your holy hill? The one whose walk is blameless, who speaks truth from the heart and has no slander on the tongue, who does his neighbour no wrong, and casts no slur on his fellow man.' Psalm 15.

Pandemic of Trespass

This is where we all have dirty hands. However much handwashing and heart wringing, we all have dirty hands.

Psalm 24, which opens with recognising that the earth is the Lord's and everything in it, a very good place to start, goes on to ask these questions: 'Who may ascend to the hill of the Lord? Who may stand in his holy place?' And the answer comes back: 'The one who has clean hands and a pure heart, who does not lift up his soul to an idol.' There is little point reading further, because that doesn't describe us. We are guilty as charged.

I have looked at my hands and they are dirty. So are yours. Look at them. This is where we all have dirty hands.

Jesus stood with some people at a hand washing place, and we have learned a lot about those places ourselves in lockdown. There was a discussion about hand washing and whether it did more than clean the hands, a bit I suppose like the saying cleanliness is next to godliness. Jesus said firmly that 'it is not what goes into your mouth that makes you dirty. It is what comes out of your mouth. For out of the heart come evil thoughts, murder, adultery, sexual immorality, theft, false testimony, slander. These are what makes a person dirty', however much you wash your hands.

We pray in the Lord's prayer, 'Forgive us our trespasses, as we forgive those who trespass against us;' but we are far happier about the first bit, our being forgiven, than the second bit, about those who have hurt us; because our forgiving is too often a reluctant thing, while we hope, at times against hope, that God's forgiving is more liberal than ours. Either way we all have dirty hands.

When King David in the Bible, himself caught in a dreadful

trespass, began to examine his own heart he found that his trespass, his sin, was deeper than ever he had imagined. He had always had it, but perhaps hadn't always been so aware of it: 'Surely I was sinful at birth, sinful from the time my mother conceived me. Now I realise my transgression, and my sin is always before me.' Psalm 51.3-6.

Isaiah the prophet, who was a great proclaimer of hope, was also a great reader of the human heart, and he declared that 'all of us have become like one who is dirty, and all our righteous acts are like filthy rags.' The prophet Jeremiah was said to be a gloomy prophet. I am not surprised because he looked at mankind without having to put his spectacles on. He said, 'the heart is deceitful above all things and beyond cure. Who can understand it?' Jeremiah 17.3.

Back to David in Psalm 51: 'Against you, Lord, you only have I sinned and done what is evil in your sight.' We are besieged with pandemics at this time. Or rather we are super conscious of pandemics at this time, health pandemics, social pandemics, political pandemics. There is also a pandemic of trespass. It has been around a long time. It is here today. It infects every generation, every culture, every hero, every mother, every one of us. Me too. You too.

The apostle Paul stated that there is no difference, no exception, no-one excluded, no-one immune from this. To quote: 'There is no difference, for all have sinned and fall short of the glory of God.' Romans 3.23. There is a pandemic of trespass. Trespass against one another. More importantly trespass against God.

Make no mistake. It is the root of all trespasses. It lies in the human heart. It is a hereditary condition. It is fuelled and fermented and spread by every influence on us, whatever our background. This is where every prejudice begins. In the human heart. It is where it all begins. The question is where does it end?

The apostle Paul wrote deeply about this in his Letter to the Romans in the New Testament, and at one point cries out – in the middle of a page – 'What a wretched man I am! Who will rescue me from this body of death?' Humbly, seriously, thoughtfully, faithfully, that is probably the best way for all of us to start. It always begins with recognition, recognition about God, recognition about ourselves. It always asks the question about the way out, or the path to forgiveness, or the road map to change, inner change, God made change.

The apostle Paul answered his own question: 'Thanks be to God – through Jesus Christ our Lord.' There is an answer, because 'God did not spare his own Son, but gave him up for us all.' Romans 7.24-5; 8.32. 'We all, like sheep, have gone astray, and turned each of us to his own way, and the Lord has laid on him the iniquity of us all' Isaiah 53.6.

This is a deep thing. We are right, so right, to get het up and ready for action against injustice. Let us man the barricades if we need to; but it is so dangerous to neglect the injustice that lies and festers in my heart.

'The wages of sin is death, but the gift of God is eternal life through Jesus Christ our Lord.' Romans 6.23.

Pandemic of Doubt

You've probably never heard of this bloke, who was a man of faith, but who lived at a time when faith seemed on the wane, and evidence for God's good hand seemed hard to find. I suspect you have known the kind of feeling. For the record, his name was Ethan the Ezrahite, and he wrote Psalm 89 in the Bible. We don't know what century BC he lived in, but we know he lived in an upside down time, when things, good things, ordered things, he and his contemporaries had taken for granted, were shoved to one side; when the world did not appear as it was meant to be, or so he thought.

He is interesting because he is like us. He begins his Psalm strongly and talks about God in the way that people of faith like to talk about God: everything is fine.

'I will sing of the Lord's great love for ever. I will declare that your love stands firm for ever.'

He goes onto describe God in the cosmos, God in nature, God in history, God in his Word, God in his essential character.

'Righteousness and justice are the foundation of your throne. Love and faithfulness go before you.'

All good so far. But then it isn't, because that is not how the world always looks. The Psalmist says that that is not how the world looks right now. It is certainly not how my world looks right now. So he asks the question. He asks the question we have all asked at some time.

'O Lord where is your former great love? How long, O Lord? Will you hide yourself for ever?' In case you're looking for the answer, Ethan doesn't give it; although he ends with a door ajar for hope: 'Praise be the Lord for ever. Amen and Amen.'

Not all of us even have the door open a teeny bit for that hope.

We have been talking of pandemics. I suggest there is another pandemic – a pandemic of doubt. It is a serious pandemic. For many of us we are stuck with Ethan's question. Many have gone beyond even asking the question, for in our society faith is very much an individual choice. You believe this, I don't. I believe this, you don't. As long as we all get along, then it is alright. If we don't get along, or someone complains about what we believe, then it's not alright, and society may intervene. That is our state of affairs currently. In that sense one's man's doubt is another's certainty, so that's alright then.

But it isn't alright. Ethan knew it wasn't alright, because faith matters. What I believe about God matters immensely. It affects how I see the world, how I understand the world. For Ethan it didn't seem to add up, but he wasn't going to let go. He was holding on until doubt once more became faith. That is why he ends his song with a double Amen.

The writer of Psalm 14 reckoned that doubt, or, beyond doubt, unbelief, is something that leads to wrong ways, wrong living: 'The fool has said in his heart: there is no God.'

The apostle Paul wrote that having a wrong belief about God can undermine everything. He might have added that having no belief about God can make for a very empty world, but no belief wasn't so much an issue for his generation; it was wrong belief. He writes: 'What may be known about God is plain. Since the creation of the world God's invisible qualities – his eternal power and divine nature – have been clearly seen, being understood, so that men and women are without excuse. (And what's worse) although they knew God, they neither glorified him as God, nor gave thanks to him, but their thinking became futile and their foolish hearts were darkened.' Romans 1.18-21.

Back to Ethan. He asked a very powerful question: 'O Lord where is your former great love?' He asked it because he knew about it. He asked it because he wanted to see it, to know it, to feel it. He was on the right track. Doubt has spread across our society, maybe our world, like a pandemic, dismissing faith as past or outdated. In truth, however, to stand in all the other pandemics of disease, of racism, of inequality, of downright oppression and unfairness, this is the one pandemic you need to resist. Ethan knew that, which is why he asked the question, and sought the answer.

There is a story in the gospels, John chapter 6, where Jesus has followed up a seriously dramatic miracle with some seriously challenging teaching; but too many of his so-called followers won't buy it. They don't like the teaching. They doubt it is for them. They shake their heads and say: 'This is a hard teaching. Who can accept it?' They vote with their feet and leave.

Jesus turns round to the handful of disciples remaining, and asks: 'Do you want to leave as well?' To which Simon Peter answers, 'Lord, where will we go? You have the words of eternal life. We believe and know that you are the Holy One of God.'

They knew it. They stuck at it. They would hold on with their faith and see it through. Because, with Ethan, they believed in God's great love.

The doubt is spreading, but the love is stronger. Know it. Stick with it. Hold on to it, to Him. Trust Him.

Use the double Amen. Amen and Amen.

Pandemic of Grace

We are learning, or being reminded, of the skeletons in so many cupboards. About flawed heroes, or perhaps about those whose flaws strip away their hero status. Being carved in stone and stood on a plinth for all to see, doesn't mean people won't see what they might not have wanted to be seen. The same of course could be said of all of us. I am tempted to pray, Lord, keep them from putting up a plaque about me, lest I appear far less than some have thought. I have been approached by some people to support a memorial seat being installed for someone in the community. A dangerous thing perhaps this memorial business.

There but for the grace of God go I. I want us to think about grace. There are many things, both good and ill, stated of many people. Of Jesus Christ it was said 'grace and truth came through him.' Now for some examples of grace.

This man was a born liar, literally as even the meaning of his name indicates deceit. He cheated his twin brother, deceived his parents, was hustled by his own uncle. He was a wheeler and dealer. But grace found him. The grace of God got hold of him and, in his case, it was like a fight. When he found that God had hold of him, he wouldn't let go of God. Flawed and favoured. The work of grace. His name was Jacob.

This woman lived on the edge of town literally. Her profession if you can call it that was prostitution, though she might have preferred to call it hospitality, because she opened her home to travellers. She lived a sort of twilight existence between different loyalties, but when she saw the work of God, she saw it for what it was, and believed it, and pleaded that God might favour her. Grace comes in unlikely places. In truth it always comes in unlikely places. Her name was Rahab.

He was just a boy, a teenager, the runt of the pack, condemned in his adolescence to take on all the menial tasks, outcast as it were to keep an eye on the family's sheep. But God said of him through the prophet that this boy was a man after God's own heart. By grace he grew as a man with a heart for God, even if his heart and his life and his actions didn't always match the accolade. Because grace was at work. His name was David.

She was a teenager, pregnant, hesitant, worried about the future, potentially and innocently facing the fearful prospects of the Law. But she knew about grace. In fact she said it of herself: 'My soul glorifies the Lord, and my spirit rejoices in God my Saviour, for he has been mindful of the humble state of his servant.' Her name was Mary.

I know a man who God has touched and grace has tempered the rage of his life. I know a woman who Christ has met and grace has given her hope. I know a man to whom faith came and grace has given him a determined life of service. I know a woman who God has touched and grace has gifted with the eye of day by day faith.

The apostle Paul wrote this: 'Even though I was once a blasphemer and a persecutor and a violent man, I was shown mercy because I acted in ignorance and unbelief. The grace of our Lord was poured out on me abundantly, along with the faith and love that are in Christ Jesus.' 1 Timothy 1.13-14.

I believe in the theory of change, but I believe in the change that comes by grace, because no other change comes in the way that grace brings it. God's grace. The apostle Paul again: 'For all have sinned and come short of the glory of God, and are justified freely by God's grace through the redemption that came by Jesus Christ.' Romans 3.23-4. Costly grace. Effective grace. Saving grace.

We have thought about pandemics - pandemics of disease, of racism, of inequality, of downright oppression and unfairness, pandemic of doubt.

But if there is one pandemic I would crave, it would be the pandemic of grace. That God would be gracious to me. That his grace would find me. That his grace would catch me and his love and peace and forgiveness and hope and strength infect me. That his grace would be 'lavished on us with all wisdom and understanding.' (Ephesians 1.8).

There is only one way to end this piece. With grace. 'Grace and peace to you from him who is and was and is to come.' Revelation 1.4. God grant us his grace.

Chapter 5: You'll never walk alone

Cup Final Day 2020

Saturday began as a bit of a dump and didn't really recover from it. I was up early gathering weeks of garden bush prunings into a couple of 'ton' bags, avoiding the piercing of thorns where I could, and stuffing them in to the back of the car. I thought that if we got to the municipal recycling centre quite soon after it opened at 7.30am, then it should be a smooth progress. At 7.40 we joined the queue and sat and shunted. At 8.50 our car had reached the entrance to the dump. At 9.50 our car had crawled the 100 further yards around the container crates and was parked in a bay to unload our prunings. At 9.55 we were on the road again. I suppose if we got used to this it might be training for the January sales, if there will ever again be January sales.

Where could we queue next? We tried B&Q. Parked easily, and joined a pedestrian line of 50 people six feet apart. That was pretty quick. We loaded a trolley with more plants, a pressure washer and some other bits. Surprising how sitting around can be so tiring. By the time we reached home it felt like breakfast had very much been missed out. Egg, sausage and mushrooms on toast. Now for the half weekly shop. To date we had not visited any supermarket during Covid-19, and today would be no different. The little Co-Op, half hidden off Norbury High Road, served us well, so we got the bits and pieces needed for a few days. Outside the shop the young man with the big smile was hovering as usual. I asked if he needed a sandwich. He declined and said it was money for the hostel he needed today. I gave him none, but hardly had I got in the shop when he dropped a bottle of blackcurrant into my trolley with his big grin.

There haven't been too many dumpish days for us over this Covid-19 period, so to have one may have been of some therapy. I almost forgot. There was a highlight to the day. There should always be a highlight in a day. Always some point of praise, some acknowledgement of grace. Some thankfulness.

Today would have been FA Cup Final day, Saturday 24th May, so a group of us gathered outside a friend's house in Balham and sang Abide with Me, just as it is always done at Wembley. Neighbours, passers by, family and friends. "Abide with me. Fast falls the eventide, the darkness deepens, Lord with me abide. When other helpers fail and comforts flee, help of the helpless, oh, abide with me."

Everton and Liverpool shirts, Chelsea and Charlton, Palace and Newcastle. All singing out their hearts. The words ever poignant, ever surprisingly set in a football context strangely out of place, and yet perhaps so clearly in place, as where better should such words of permanency in a transient world be sung than in the nation's greatest choir, that of a football crowd.

"Hold thou thy cross before my closing eyes. Shine through the gloom and point me to the skies. Heaven's morning breaks and earth's dark shadows flee. In life, in death, O Lord, abide with me."

There wasn't much singing during Covid 2020, so this chapter is about singing.

Swing low sweet chariot

I want to sing. The sun is going to shine and singing would be a good thing. The Premier league re-started which could be another opportunity for crowd anthems, except that it wasn't. I don't think it as easy to sing from the sofa at home 'I'm for ever blowing bubbles, pretty bubbles in the air', but West Ham supporters might just have to settle for watching the bubble machine at the side of the pitch instead, and from the comfort of the living room. Nor is it so easy to chant, 'You don't know what you're doing', or other essential jibes at referee or manager, or some dedicated rhymes to a favoured player from the comfort of the sitting room. The beautiful game came back, but without the camaraderie of the terraces.

I find it interesting how some of these indispensable sports songs, bellowed out so lustily at great events are songs with a spiritual, if not heavenly meaning. In this chapter I want to sing some of them. Well, not exactly sing them, as even the pigeons might complain.

In this time of questioning, the anthems in the stands are the subject of investigation. There is a thought that Rugby fans will be asked not to sing 'swing low, sweet chariot,' because it is too glib a repetition of a song of struggle far removed from Twickenham, a heart felt song coming out of the American slave experience. Boris says don't stop singing it, but apparently he didn't recall any of the words after the first sentence. That is half the problem with these songs. To twist the football chant: you don't know what you're singing.

Apparently, the song was introduced to the 'rugby fraternity' as early as 1960 by a folk singer, who had heard the great Paul Robeson sing it; which is from whom I probably heard it first on a radio; but there are different stories as to how it was brought into rugby crowds from the late eighties. It is a song of hope in struggle, developed by African American slaves to lament their tribulations, probably sung with reference to the Underground Railway that led so many to freedom, but freedom through danger. It is thought to have been composed by Wallis Willis from Choctaw County, Oklahoma, as early as the American Civil War, and has been sung over and over again, as a song of freedom, of struggle, of hope, of spiritual belief.

All far from the beery singing of an English rugby crowd. Either way it would be better if people knew what they were singing about. Maybe without that knowledge they shouldn't sing it. Or maybe they should sing it with a bit of understanding.

Maybe they should also know the Bible origin and inspiration of the song.

The life and work of the great Old Testament prophet, Elijah, was at its close. Accompanied by his disciple Elisha, he was walking towards his own exodus, with a growing crowd of curious observers. When they reached the river Jordan, the crowd kept its distance, and watched as Elijah took his cloak, rolled it up, and struck the water, which miraculously parted. He and Elisha walked across on dry ground. The waters flowed again behind them. Elijah looked his young disciple in his face and asked what can I do for you before I am taken away. Without a blink, the disciple said to the master, 'Let me inherit a double portion of your spirit.' To which Elijah said that he better watch with all the watching he possessed, if he wanted that gift.

'As they were walking along and talking together, suddenly a chariot of fire and horses of fire appeared and separated the two of them, and Elijah went up to heaven in a whirlwind. Elisha saw this and cried out: "My father! My Father! The chariots and horsemen of Israel!" And Elisha saw him no more.'

Wow! No wonder, Wallis Willis wrote: Swing low, sweet chariot, Coming for to carry me home. And sung it as a song of freedom, of struggle, of hope, of spiritual belief. No wonder it has been sung over and again in times of protest and aspiration and perseverance and campaigning. Strange though that it has been sung at rugby matches, but perhaps there is something to be learnt even there.

"I looked over Jordan and what did I see, Coming for to carry me home.

A band of angels coming after me.

Swing low, sweet chariot, Coming for to carry me home.

If you get there before I do, Tell all my friends I'm coming too, Coming for to carry me home.

Swing low, sweet chariot, Coming for to carry me home."

When Elisha caught that sight of the chariots of fire and the disappearance of the prophet, he felt that things would never be the same again for him. It was a hinge moment. He took his own clothes and tore them apart and threw them down. He picked up the cloak that had fallen from Elijah and strode to the river Jordan, and struck it with Elijah's coat, shouting, 'Where now is the Lord, the God of Elijah?' and the waters parted, and he crossed over.

The mantle of the great prophet had indeed fallen on the young man to lead his own generation. The song from Elijah's story is about hope. Hope that God brings, and being carried towards that hope. It is also about heaven, and the hope that God brings. That through all today's hardships, there is a tomorrow. There is a God given tomorrow. Willis didn't, as far as is known, sing about the Elisha part of the story, though perhaps he might have been tempted to sing of those who are still here, finding their own path in their generation. He might have been tempted to find words for those on whose shoulders falls the mantle of leadership, whose task it is to take the legacy forward. For those men and women brave enough to ask, indeed demand, a double portion of the Elijah spirit of leadership. Bold, full of faith, undivided in perseverance, holding tenaciously to truth and God given values.

It is a hard prayer to pray. It is a necessary prayer to pray, though not all can pray it. I wonder who there is who can pray it for their generation, while onlookers hesitate, afraid to boldly go, and firmly stand. I wonder who can pray it in this generation, and with eyes closely fixed, believe it and watch.

'Lord, let me inherit a double portion of your spirit.' (2 Kings 2).

Those feet in ancient time

So the Barmy Army didn't stand proud at Lord's in the summer, with arms outraised and singing at the tops of their voices, 'And did those feet in ancient time walk upon England's mountains green,' because the cricket tests were played in front of empty stands. West Indian cricket coach, Phil Simmons, had said that perhaps that would give his team an edge, to play without the cacophony of English voices swaying across the green pitch.

Jerusalem is another of those anthems sung at sporting events, whose meaning probably passes by many of those who sing it, but who nevertheless feel the better for howling it out. I used to think it was a daft song, with improbable lines as 'and was the holy Lamb of God on England's pleasant pastures seen.' I used to think it, until I realised that William Blake, the poet, who wrote it long before cricket was played at the Oval, was exploring something deeper.

It is a good question to ask whether God can be found where there is darkness, or struggle; whether Christ can make his home in a place where what is natural seems to be torn apart, or squashed and buried: 'And did the Countenance Divine shine forth upon our clouded hills? And was Jerusalem builded here among those dark Satanic Mills.' Equally there is something impressive about the determination to secure change that is for the better, to bring about a better tomorrow, to work towards Christ's day in our land: 'I will not cease from Mental Fight, nor shall my Sword sleep in my hand: till we have built Jerusalem, in England's green & pleasant Land.'

Space is too short to even begin to scratch the surface of what Blake was talking about, at the outset of the industrial revolution in Britain, but suffice to say that everybody has sung it, since Parry and Elgar combined to make it like a national anthem during the first world war. The suffragettes used it big time. The Labour Party used to sing it along with keeping the red flag flying high.

Numerous rock bands have incorporated a version of it in their shows. It was sung at Will and Kate's wedding. And we will keep singing it.

The song even cross references to swing low sweet chariot, that we thought of already, as both songs take some inspiration from the prophet Elijah, and his chariots, with the words 'bring me my chariot of fire.' But whatever the song is about, it is about a prophetic voice in the world, about not keeping silent, when something should be said. In an early version of Blake's poem, he has inscribed as a footnote some words of Moses, from the book of Numbers, in the Old Testament: 'I wish that all the Lord's people were prophets and that the Lord would put his Spirit upon them.' Numbers 11.29. Moses' right hand man, Joshua, had come to him with a complaint, that a couple of the men hadn't come into the tabernacle, but were prophesying outside. Joshua wanted permission to shut them up, but Moses with a sigh laments that there were not more prophets: I wish that all the Lord's people were prophets.

That is a question for today. Where are the prophetic voices in the church, in society? Where are those who would bring God's word as sharp and true and challenging for today? Who will go to the moral armoury, impassioned, and demand, 'Bring me my bow of burning gold, bring me my Arrows of desire. Bring me my Spear! O clouds unfold, bring me my Chariot of Fire!'

The apostle Paul wrote, 'Pray for us that God may open a door for our message, so that we may proclaim the mystery of Christ. Pray that I may proclaim it clearly as I should.' Colossians 4.3.

It was said of the prophet Samuel's youth, that 'In those days the word of the Lord was rare. There were not many visions.' 1 Samuel 3.1. Perhaps so today. Along with Moses and with Blake we might say, I wish that all the Lord's people were prophets. And then pray for those feet to walk here.

Abide with me

So we didn't get to go to Wembley, and we didn't get to sing along to Abide with me, as it has been sung at pretty well every final since 1927.

This is another of our sporting anthems, that we sing with gusto, but that to us are often short of meaning; often sung without really thinking what is being said. Strange too that what is essentially a song for funerals, is sung at a celebration of life. Strange that a song composed by Henry Francis Lyte in the last months of his struggle with tuberculosis, and that helped him and others, and countless others since, focus on their last days, should be sung in an arena to extol full, young and athletic strength. Certainly a contrast from what they used to sing in earlier cup finals. Prior to 1927, for many years the band struck up with: 'Come on and hear, come on and hear, Alexander's Ragtime Band. Come on and hear, come on and hear, 'bout the best band in the land.' I can certainly see why they wanted such an up tempo start to a football fest; but they changed it for something more thoughtful, more serious, and as it has proved more lasting. Perhaps it is because the powers that be realised that something was needed that was less ephemeral, more significant, than ninety minutes of kicking a ball around. Or perhaps, realising that to many football is life, there should be something sung that reflected the ebb and flow of 'life's little day.' Perhaps, prophetically they anticipated that what would be the greatest global connector needed something equally connecting, that also links us all together: that sense of earth's passing glories, and the 'change and decay in all around I see, but Thou who changest not, abide with me.'

But I think that as with most songs, we remember the beginning, and often the beginning is sufficient for us. I suspect that the moment of reflection at the beginning of the game, for player and spectator alike, is meaningful. That sense of togetherness, of needing others. That worry about aloneness, and needing companions. That sense of weakness and needing strength. The words are incomparable: 'Abide with me. Fast falls the eventide. The darkness deepens, Lord with me abide. When other helpers fail, and comforts flee, help of the helpless, O abide with me.'

No matter who we are, we have sung or said or prayed those words, or similar words – 'when other helpers fail, and comforts flee, help of the helpless.' We have all known a time when we have reached out or wanted to reach out. Some have known a time when reaching out seemed in vain, and we appeared alone, with only ourselves to be our help. There is an encyclopaedia in those few words of empathy and sympathy and indeed pathos. There is a strength too and a resolution. Long may it be sung at Wembley. Long may it be sung at funerals. A pity it is not more sung in churches, because it is song of deep hope. It is a spiritual song. It is a Christian song.

It is a song about everyday faith: 'I need Thy presence every passing hour.' It is a song about trust in struggle: 'What but thy grace can foil the tempter's power?' It is a song about direction: 'Who like thyself my guide and stay can be?' It is above all a song about the presence and companionship of Christ, rain or shine: 'Through cloud and sunshine, O abide with me.'

It is said, that in the summer of 1847, Henry Lyte, having preached a farewell sermon to his congregation in Brixham, Devon, by the seaside, that he went home into his study, and wrote the words of Abide with me, and composed a tune to go with it. He gave it to his daughter, and made arrangements to travel to the south of France in the hope of respite for his medical condition; but died within two weeks. Apparently he had often thought about those simply profound or profoundly simple words of Jesus, Abide with me, but now was the time to put in words something of what they meant to him.

'I fear no foe with Thee at hand to bless. Ills have no weight and tears no bitterness. Where is death's sting? Where grave, thy victory? I triumph still if Thou abide with me.'

Oh, for more of that enduring faith, that transcends all generations, all situations.

Jesus said to his disciples on the night of his betrayal: 'Abide in me, and I will abide in you.' John 15.4.

Guide me O Thou great Jehovah

The question is perhaps when Welsh voices will sing as one, in harmony, 'bread of heaven, bread of heaven, feed me till I want no more, want no more' and that rising crescendo of sound will stir up partisan and spectator alike. Of all the sports anthems we have thought about, this one makes the most sense. Derived from a hymn by the great eighteenth century Welsh Methodist preacher, William Williams of Pantycelyn, it reflects something of a deep national spirituality, that although somewhat past, is nevertheless close enough to historical memories.

Needless to say that British football crowds have subverted the tune of the chorus to regularly taunt opponents with 'You're not singing anymore' or more supportively, 'We'll support you ever more'; but in truth it is the former that I have heard more regularly from the terraces. Strange to me that men who would barely mumble the words of a hymn, if they find themselves unusually inside a church, will bellow out along with the mainly male voice choir of the terraces. I suppose in a way the football arena, or sporting arena, has become the church – the place of fellowship and identity, the place where passion and affection can be expressed in equal measure, where the restraints are relaxed and a man or indeed woman can shout out things they probably wouldn't in their grandmother's hearing. However apart from those great sporting occasions where the great songs are sung the lyrics at football crowds are pretty basic, pretty banal, and often only half sung. Strange too those temples of camaraderie stand silent for now.

Back to bread of heaven, it is a great Christian hymn of pilgrimage through this life, a prayer for God's guiding, strengthening, providing hand: it begins with the words 'Guide me O Thou great Jehovah.' It is a song asking and trusting God to do something exceptional in our life journeys, to open the fountain of the healing stream, to shine the fire to light the way, to lead us from start to finish: 'Strong deliverer, be Thou still my strength and shield.' And, of course, it is a prayer about God's help in facing death, which captures so closely what we will all one day feel: 'When I tread the verge of Jordan, bid my anxious fears subside.' You can sense the tension and the concern in the words, followed then by some of the most powerful assured words in hymnody: 'Death of death, and hell's destruction, land me safe on Canaan's side.'

William Williams, of course, wrote in Welsh. Indeed he preached in Welsh, and wrote and published many songs and poems in Welsh, that had a profound effect on eighteenth century Welsh faith. The English version we have has been through a number of iterations to get to where it is now, but as it is, has lasted, and we still sing it, whether in the great arenas or in little churches, and this song continues to stir and strengthen faith.

It is fitting that it is sung at sports occasions. Long may it do so. It is a powerful thing for a man or woman of little or no belief to sing these words. It is a powerful thing for a man or woman of faith to sing these words. It is a powerful thing to sing these words and reflect on their meaning and how they connect to this life journey of ours. It is a powerful thing to pray it as a prayer today. Now.

'Guide me, O Thou great Jehovah, pilgrim through this barren land. I am weak, but Thou art mighty. Hold me with Thy powerful hand. Bread of heaven, feed me now and evermore.' Amen.

Arglwydd, arwain trwy'r anialwch.

God save the Queen

Yes, when the National Anthem is sung, I do usually stand to attention in the living room or wherever I am, and respectfully consider the words 'God save our gracious Queen.' I do it as expression of nationhood, of belonging to this diverse and historic land. I do it out of respect to the Queen as a person, and the notion of government and collaboration and order and of peace. I do it in recognition that she as a head of state and we as a people are acknowledging our need of God's help.

I notice that it is sung at less and less occasions. For example other songs accompany national sporting events. I notice too that over the centuries it has had some very different verses added or taken away. I suppose that makes sense because the national story has been a bit up and down. In the early days of the song there was a version to encourage the English against the Scots, and vice versa, the Scots against the English, in the time of King George II and bonny Prince Charlie. There have been verses that sung about protection from assassins. There has often been included a verse about scattering the enemies, sometimes up front and shall we say aggressive: "Scatter our enemies, and make them fall! Confound their politics, frustrate their knavish tricks. On Thee our hopes we fix, God save us all!"

Sometimes changing the ideas somewhat as with this version: 'O Lord Our God Arise, scatter her enemies, make wars to cease. Keep us from plague and dearth, turn thou our woes to mirth;

And over all the earth let there be peace.'

Of course, the bottom line in all this, in fact the top line as well, is that it is a prayer for the nation. In whatever version you have, there is God save. God save the king or queen, God save us, God save us all. But always God save. In April 2007, there was an amendment to an early day motion in the House of Commons proposing that the song chosen for English sporting occasions "should have a bit more oomph than God save the Queen and should also not involve God." I suppose that is the rub. Does the nation want to acknowledge God? Does the nation want prayer to be a part of national life? Clearly with every passing decade as a nation we loosen our faith links, and increasingly approach the point where the God words are becoming empty. But we are not there yet. Certainly the Queen herself does what she can to frame the nation in a spiritual context. Politicians on the other hand tend to use words like prayer and God but almost casually.

For that reason alone, I will continue to sing when occasion arises, 'God save our gracious Queen, long live our noble Queen, God save the Queen.' If opportunity comes, I will happily sing, "Thy choicest gifts in store, on her be pleased to pour. May she defend our laws, and ever give us cause, to sing with heart and voice, God save the Queen!" I will also, following the lead of the apostle Paul, pray 'for kings and all those in authority, that we may live peaceful and quiet lives in all godliness and holiness. For this is good, and pleases God our Saviour, who wants all to be saved and come to a knowledge of the truth: that there is one God and one mediator between God and man, the man Christ Jesus, who gave himself as a ransom for all.' 1 Timothy 2.1-6.

In 1836, William Hickson added this verse, which was used in the Queen's Golden Jubilee in 2002, and sung at the 2008 Olympics closing ceremony. It is a prayer:

'Not in this land alone, but be God's mercies known from shore to shore:

Lord, make the nations see that men should brothers be, and from one family the wide world o'er.' Amen.

Never walk alone

There was been music and singing everywhere in the Lockdown summer. Rappers on a van in west London, until they were moved on. Reggae music in a park in Battersea, while quiet groups barbecued and talked, until the rain dampened it a bit. Impromptu summer music in other places. Despite government warnings, it was always going to be hard to keep people penned in as the sunshine insistently beckoned. Please God there was neither a spike in Covid cases, nor a continuing spike in social tensions at that time. Of course, the one celebration that would be most impatient of confined and discreet rejoicing, took place in Liverpool, as long into the night there was singing and making noise to celebrate the final victory in the Premiership after thirty years of waiting. If you follow football, however partisan you are, you cannot begrudge the success of this exceptional team.

Surely without debate the best, most telling, most meaningful, most purposeful football song is 'You'll never walk alone'. Doubtless sung that night in Liverpool until voices were too hoarse to sing any more, the song touches a courage and pathos and connection to many years of human story connected to that football club and that city. It is their song.

"When you walk through a storm hold your head up high, and don't be afraid of the dark.

At the end of a storm there's a golden sky and the sweet silver song of a lark.

Walk on through the wind, walk on through the rain, though your dreams be tossed and blown

Walk on, walk on, with hope in your heart, and you'll never walk alone"

I, of course, would have sung along to those words as a teenager, listening to Gerry and the Pacemakers, but I doubt at the time I would have realised that the origin of the song came from the pen of Rodgers and Hammerstein and their musical "Carousel". I looked up where the song sits in the story, and it is quite poignant. Nettie Fowler sings the song to support her cousin, Julie, whose husband Billy has fallen on his knife, fatally after a failed robbery. In the grief of the moment, Julie feels so alone, and then comes the song – walk on with hope in your heart. Not easy to do at such a time. The relevance of these words never seems to fade.

To walk alone is a hard step. Avoid it. Avoid it as much as possible. Find a friend. If you can't find a friend, find a stranger. Talk with someone. Talking helps the journey.

I received this email about someone I have known for many years. This is what the email said: "He is in a very bad place at the moment. Said he has tried to commit suicide 3 times. Once by walking into a lorry - he has lost nearly all his bottom teeth - and once from a bridge where a member of the public pulled him back. He is very depressed and opened up after a while to how difficult and horrible his life is at the moment. He has been severely affected by Corona losing significant weekly income and is having a hard time in his personal life as well. He was very negative but, I think, just wants normal nice people to be able to talk to and listen to him. He's had a hard life with some big issues and traumas. I encouraged him to keep believing and said I would pray for him to which he replied don't bother I'm an atheist. But I said I would anyway."

Don't walk alone. Look out for those who are walking alone. Be willing to talk with strangers. Always smile or greet or nod at people you pass. Connect. Always connect. The preacher in the Book of Ecclesiastes wrote: 'Two are better than one. If one falls down, his friend can help him up. But pity the one who falls and has no-one to help him up. Though one be overpowered, two can defend themselves. A cord of three strands is not easily broken.' Ecclesiastes 4.9-12. We know what the third strand is. Hold on to it.

'Yea, though I walk through the valley of the shadow of death, I will fear no evil; for thou art with me. Your rod and your staff they comfort me.' Psalm 23.4.

"Walk on through the wind, walk on through the rain, though your dreams be tossed and blown. Walk on, walk on, with hope in your heart, and you'll never walk alone"

Chapter 6: After the Fire

Until it pass. Lockdown summer

I then turned to my Bible, and read these words: 'Have mercy on me, O God, have mercy on me, for in you my soul takes refuge. I will take refuge in the shadow of your wings, until the disaster has passed.' Psalm 57.1.

That I guess is what we have all been asked to do. Lie low until this business is all over and it is safe to come out and mingle again. Or for those who daily go out with their work, whatever it is, to keep their safe distances, until this thing has passed. Or for those in front line care services, to wear the protective equipment, to act with that delicate combination of care for the patient with care for oneself. Until the disaster has passed.

If you look at the heading of Psalm 57, you will notice that David, the Psalmist, wasn't writing, or indeed singing, about a virus outbreak, or any such thing. He was on the run for his life. The half-deranged monarch, King Saul, was after him with an army, seeking his life; while David and his band of brothers, eluded him, forever on the run. The note for this Psalm says it has a music title – 'Do not destroy' – which would make a pertinent title for our own songs at this time. Then it refered to the occasion that inspired David to write it: "When he had fled from Saul into a cave." The caves around En Gedi, in the hills above the Dead Sea, are deep enough to hide more than a handful of refugees.

David's plan was to hide in the cave, and try and stick it out until the danger had passed. He goes on in this Psalm to describe his enemies like a pride of ferocious lions, with teeth like spears and arrows, and tongues like sharp swords. Definitely a danger to keep away from, and wait until danger has passed. If hunkering down until the trouble had passed, and staying within a safe place, was all the Psalmist was saying, that in itself could resonate for us. But he, of course, was saying something more. Yes, of course, I want to come out of this in one piece, free to go where I wish, free to mingle with my friends and family without restriction. Yes, of course, I want to emerge as fit as when I went into lockdown, hiding in this cave.

But there is something deeper here. He says that his refuge isn't a cave. His place of safety is God. You, O Lord, are my refuge. It is Your mercy and grace that I seek, not just for my body, not just for my mind; but also for my soul, my whole being. The place I need to be is where You keep me safe, in the shadow of Your wings. It is that place of heart safety. That place of faith safety. That place of trust safety. That place of belonging safety. My enemies might drag me out of this cave, but not from that place of soul safety. This present trouble might diminish me bodily, but please God not diminish me within.

After the fire

Cosmo — at least that is what I think he calls himself — is no longer living rough. He has been swept up along with many homeless to stay for now in a Travel Lodge. He still has to live, so he has done a bit of begging, perhaps repeatedly. He got arrested and spent the night in a cell. For now, perhaps no longer homeless, but still hungry. Rachel lives on the tenth floor with six children. Something in the self-isolation cracked and she could take no more, and broke the curfew and moved in with a relation. Probably no more space but a bit of a garden, and maybe some mental space. Grace works in the hospital and says that of the twenty who have been in intensive care with this virus, only one has survived to date.

Now we are beginning to ask, what will happen on the other side. What will happen after the fire?

Justin Welby in his Easter message had said that "That sense of a new direction and intention, of hope that carries us forward, is likely to be mocked by many. Cynicism tells us that all will go on as before. Despair tells us that the road is coming to an end. Fear tells us to look after ourselves. Imaginative hope gives us a level-headed courage and a grand ambition, when it is based on what we know to be true."

He is not the only one to warn against dangers of normality, of the slide towards greater disparity and injustice. He went onto say: "There will still be wickedness and war, poverty and persecution, greed and grasping. There always has been; always will be. Yet in the resurrection of Jesus Christ God lights a fire which calls us to justice, to live in humble generosity, to transform our societies. After so much suffering, so much heroism across the globe, once this epidemic is conquered here and elsewhere, we cannot be content to go back to what was before as if all was normal. There needs to be a resurrection of our common life, a new normal, something that links to the old, but is different and more beautiful. We must dream it, build it, make it, grasp it, because it is the gift of God and the call of God."

That for me is the rub. Will there be a collective will for change? Will economic and social choices or no choices drop us into a different kind of pestilence. There is a nervous looking ahead. We can at least begin with ourselves. In the words of the apostle Peter: 'Therefore be clear minded and self-controlled so that you can pray. Above all, love each other deeply, because love covers a multitude of sins. Offer hospitality to one another without grumbling. Each one should use whatever gift he has received to serve others. If anyone speaks, he should do it as speaking the very words of God. If anyone serves, he should to it with all the strength God provides, so that in all things God may be praised through Jesus Christ. To him be the glory and the power for ever. Amen.' 1 Peter 4.7-11.

The Proof

One night I had turned the radio on and half listened to Any Questions. A lady put this question to the panel. Did they think that the Corona Virus epidemic proves that God does not exist? I only half listened so I can only half remember what was said. One panel member replied that from what she remembered from studies years before, the question of suffering didn't feature in the standard proofs for the existence of God, and went on to talk about the importance of faith in hard times and the positive role that people of faith play in such periods. Another panel member, I recall, reckoned this was the wrong question to ask, and again at times like this faith and hope are big factors in well-being and coping.

I'm afraid I didn't stay to hear Archbishop John Sentamu's response as a panel member, but he had earlier issued a joint statement with Justin Welby: "Where is our hope? It is in the end in the love and faithfulness of a God whom we may have forgotten, but whose action and character is expressed in millions of acts of love by every person in this country. This is the God who we see in Jesus Christ, who called himself the Good Shepherd. Acts of love are the normal reaction to those in need. They are a reflection of the God who is our Shepherd."

I suppose the questioner was either wanting someone to say something along the lines, that if this thing is of God, then what kind of God is he? Or if God is so powerful then why has he not stopped it, thus proving he isn't there anyway? Or maybe she was wanting to hear something real, because she had heard too many platitudes, of fine words but empty of reality and hope.

One night I accompanied a woman of faith, driving around to deliver food parcels in various parts of Battersea, until it got too late to take any more. To the elderly man on the seventh floor, who cannot get out, and who receives his gift with tears. To the elderly lady on the second floor balcony, whose operation has been put off indefinitely, full of appreciation, but most weeks spends most of the conversation saying, that she can't eat this or that. To the large, pallid man confined to his small flat in a high-rise block, who looks like he would struggle to cope with walking outdoors anyway. To the person in the terraced house who doesn't come to the door but shouts from an upstairs room to say please leave the box outside. To the lady with a handful of kids who seems to be struggling at the best of times, and who chatted at the door, as the town fox slunk past and slipped through the fence.

I think I am with the Archbishop, who said that 'It is in the end in the love and faithfulness of a God whom we may have forgotten, but whose action and character is expressed in millions of acts of love by every person in this country.'

But I want to bring up another thought. I agree with the questioner to the panel in one sense, who I suspect is fed up with easy talk and easy faith. As I have been working my way along the Psalms in the Bible during Covid Lockdown, I am repeatedly struck by how faith is forged in adversity. How faith shines as a light in darkness, rather than as an easy choice for easy times. And given that, how more powerful and more authentic the utterances of faith appear. Here is someone who believes and who also knows about the hurt in life. Here is one who speaks out of experience about life and also about God, about God in life, about God in his life.

Here is my authentic faith quote, from Psalm 61. 'From the ends of the earth I call to you' – you see, it doesn't matter where we are from, what place, what background. Wherever, whoever, we may call on Him.

'I call as my heart grows faint' – you see, it isn't always easy. Sometimes it is downright hard. Sometimes we can barely breathe, sometimes we can barely believe.

'Lead me to the rock that is higher than I.' – that is such an extraordinary sentence, such an authentic expression. You see, we cannot find the answers inside. We cannot find the answers around us. Because they are not there. We will be looking in the wrong place, just as the women in the Easter story, who looked for Christ in the tomb. Why on earth would the Saviour of the world still be in a tomb, when he was risen, when of course he was risen!

It is to the rock that is higher than I that I must look. It is above not within. It is up not around. It is to God I should be looking – at this time, at any time. To God in Christ.

'From the ends of the earth I call to you. I call as my heart grows faint. Lead me to the rock that is higher than I.' Psalm 61.2.

New Day

I went to Mitcham Common one morning to see the sun rise in the distance between the steel masts at Crystal Palace and Norwood. It was going to be a good day. There was no-one else about, except a man and a dog who was more interested in me than following his master, a couple of men with big cameras by the lake, a couple who veered away to keep their social distance, and a man with a bag off to work.

A pair of swans, in flight, calling, their long white necks stretching forward. I stood on the hilltop towards the pink sun, with the sound of woodland birds around me, the stands of alkanet blue and damp, and cow parsley, nodding creamy white in the early breeze, the scent fresh with the morning. I read from Hine's great hymn: 'When through the woods and forest glades I wander and hear the birds sing sweetly in the trees. When I look down from lofty mountain grandeur, and hear the brook, and feel the gentle breeze, then sings my soul, my Saviour God, to thee – how great thou art! How great thou art!'

A pair of Muscovies by the lake, coughing around me with their husky call. Geese crash landing on the pond as if showing off with great splashes of water. Mallards and coots busy with morning foraging, and a clutch of ducklings, bobbing, and ducking, soft, and spotty, and eager for life. Curiously some magpies. I always seem to see magpies near the water fowl. On the lookout for something I suppose that someone else has found.

The blackthorn and cherry have faded on these meadows, and the may has barely begun to shine white and send out its sweet spring smell. The rabbits were finishing from the night shift and disappearing underground. A water rat or something grey and thin tailed rustled and slipped among the low foliage near the trees by the lake.

Over all the years I have lived in this area, I never thought much of Mitcham Common, but in these days of needing to find places for a short walk, and keep within the guidelines, I have discovered what I have always been told, what a gem of nature it is. Never far from road and house and sound of traffic, it is a natural haven that has kept its social distance and flourished. The birds are settled here and sing out the length of the lengthening days. The white comfrey and the blue borage and delicate cowslips are showing now.

There is something renewing and restoring to the inner self of any patch of growing. The garden, the edge of the park, by the road side, on the housing estate. Nature will always express itself, and to see it wherever it is a sight worth seeing.

Back to the hilltop and the sweep of grassland, and the trees by the slope, and the sun now settled for the day, illuminating the housing estates of Pollard Hill, and onto Mitcham to the one hand and Croydon towards the other, and another verse from Stuart

Hine, to put the day in perspective.

'And when I think that God his Son not sparing, sent him to die – I scarce can take it in, that on the cross, my burden gladly bearing, he bled and died to take away my sin: The sings my soul, my Saviour God to thee, how great thou art! How great thou art.'

It is Sunday now, and we will not be going to church, but we will meet together. We will not be going to a building, but we will be where Christ is and he where we are; because his promise is ever renewed, that where two or three are gathered in his name, there I am.

And that promise declared from a hill, a very different hill than the mound at Mitcham Common, but a hill all the same, and an announcement, unconfined by time and place and vagaries of our human journeyings and fate:

Jesus said: 'And surely, I am with you always, to the very end of the age.' Matthews 28.20.

Beyond my thoughts

Death in Lockdown. A handful of dirt thrown into the pit. One by one, quietly, thoughtfully. More handfuls of dirt. The soft grains caught in the breeze, some falling on the casket with a light tap. Earth to earth, ashes to ashes, dust to dust.

We live in unusual times, when even the ordinary things of life, and of death, have to be done in a different way. Mourners, in their Sunday best, at a distance, some closer than others to the grave, to each other. Some stood on the bank away but within earshot. Others scattered along the path or among the other gravestones on the bright green grass. The matriarch of the family seated away from it all, ninety five years old but refusing not to be present. The wife of the deceased standing alone, singing with all

74

her heart, moving with the rhythm from foot to foot, in time with the reggae lilt of 'How great thou art', broadcast from a car's speakers – because there were no chapel services today.

The may blossom shining in the spring sunshine provided the flowers for the funeral, and the stiff breeze sweeping across the cemetery the organ. 'For He knows what of what we are made. He remembers that we are dust. Our days are like the grass. We flourish like a flower of the field; when the wind blows over it, it is gone and its place will know it no more. But the merciful goodness of the Lord lasts for ever and ever towards those that fear him, and his righteousness on their children's children.'

Covid-19 has robbed us of many things. It has also robbed us of time. Time to mourn and time to remember. But with the hope that on another day family and friends will meet again to remember shared times. For this life of threescore years and ten there were twenty minutes of dignity, of comfortable and thoughtful words, of familiar faces, two minutes of eulogy, and prayer. O Lord we have entrusted this our brother to God's mercy.

The car speakers rang out with the lyrics of Delroy Wilson: "I just wanna say Thank you. For the many things you've done, for having faith in me more than anyone."

For all, it was about tears and loss, it was about family, about standing together, although standing apart. It was about all our yesterdays, but it was about our tomorrows. About the ones who are left to continue with their own journeys. It was about a recognition that our lives are lived in the sight of God, and a gratitude for the gift that has been given.

I was there not as family except for that day, but to take the service by the grave in God's good spring air. It is a tiring thing this dying, and soul weary too.

There was to be no customary in filling of the grave by the mourners. New regulations restricted that task to the JCB. But the two sons, the wife and a brother, took lumps of London clay and broke them, as if sacramentally and dropped them on the casket.

The last sound, the last touch, the last feel of the shared earth where foot had trod.

From the car audio drifted the voice of Sanchez: "How marvellous the grace that caught my falling soul. He looked beyond my thoughts and saw my needs. Amazing grace shall always be my song of praise for it was grace that brought me liberty. And I'll never know just why Christ came to love me so. He looked beyond my thoughts and saw my need."

Chapter 7: Stretch the borders of life

'Stretch the borders of life'. Not so easy as it sounds, when there is hustle and hassle at the borders and quarantine when you've passed through them. But too much confinement is pushing us to stretch those borders.

'Stretch the borders of life'. That's what we were trying to do one week in August. Five inner city, housing estate lads, and we were off to Dartmoor, to East Shallowford Farm. That will stretch the borders of these young lives. To see the calf that was born yesterday, suckling from its mother in the field. To see the hills, and the space, when the only hills they usually see are called tower blocks. We want to literally stretch the borders of their life experience. We want them to make connections they might not be making.

Truth is we need to 'Stretch the borders of life' for ourselves, that openness, that newness, that richness.

'Stretch the borders of life'. I have borrowed this title from a heading in The Message Bible, that precedes Isaiah chapter 26. It is a beautiful chapter, but also a tough chapter of writing.

"At that time, this song will be sung in the country of Judah:

We have a strong city, Salvation City, built and fortified with salvation.

Throw wide the gates so good and true people can enter.

People with their minds set on you, you keep completely whole, steady on their feet, because they keep at it and don't quit.

Depend on God and keep at it because in the Lord God you have a sure thing." Isaiah 26.1-4.

Stretch the borders of our experience

We said we were going to the stretch the borders of their lives. To stretch the borders of their experience.

Perhaps we did a little. A little stretch to touch and see and smell the things they do not usually do. They watched the calf gingerly make its first steps on the grass towards mother. A new mother, not too sure what all this was about. The calf suckled. That was a good thing.

They caught a glimpse of the grey wings of the owl in flight late afternoon as we watch the cows in the field close by, the great bull, all quiet power, and firm muscle, looking back. We will help the farmer move them all, plus the several hundred sheep, who we had seen at night scattered like a multitude of dots in the field adjacent to the moor. We explored the moor a bit too, the bracken high, the gorse sparkling yellow, and felt and smelt and saw a different kind of landscape.

From the prophet Isaiah in the Message translation: 'The path of right-living people is level. The Leveller evens the road for the right-living. We're in no hurry, God. We're content to linger in the path sign-posted with your decisions.' Isaiah 26.7. From a more traditional rendering: 'The path of the righteous is level, O Upright One. O Lord, you make the way of the righteous smooth. Walking in the ways of your Word, we wait for You.' Isaiah 26.7 (NIV).

Lord, for ourselves. Stretch the borders of our experience, of our obedience, of our following.

Stretch the borders of our imagination

South Milton sands, very different from Brighton beach. Very different for that matter from Surrey Lane Estate. Very different from the usual for these children. That is why we were there, with that long, seemingly endless winding drive, down narrow lanes in the South Hams area of Devon. We, of course, weren't the only ones, the beach being a huge playground of sand and sea, and digging in the sand, and giggling with the sea, and children and parents on kayaks, and boards, and inflatables. And the curve of the bay, the hills to the east and west enfolding the scene like great arms of fields and cliffs.

We were there for fun, but also to stretch the borders of our imagination. To see and feel and touch and be among something more than the ordinary. Despite the wasps, on their end of season hunting for sweetness as the summer flowers have faded. We didn't pay them too much attention, and got on with the business of getting wet.

At South Milton the low tide reveals a scattered line of sharp jagged rocks that lead out towards a great stack of hardstone, rising from the water, that remains defiant whatever the tide. Among the rocks are countless little pools, and eddies of water, and as the tide slides back in on the turn, floating shapes of marine vegetation slide past on the current. Mermaid's tresses with their dark green strands, bladder wracks, brown and bulbous. Crabs scurrying under the shadows away from danger, burying themselves into the sand. Compass jellyfish, floating like parachutes on the water, brown dots in a circle, brown tentacles, and watched with care by children as they drift past on the tide.

The tide covers all. All the strip of rocks that have resisted eons of savage weathering. All the rock pools where children hunt and search. All the sand, shingle and coloured stones, striped and spotted, smooth and rough, washed here from every point of the compass. All is covered except the durable stack of rock, unmoved by tide or storm, or human connivance or man's deceit. It has been here ever since man has walked his dog along this beach. It will be here tomorrow and next year and probably until the end of time.

As the late afternoon sun glistens on the bay, the brown green rock stands above the waves, firm, upright, almost as if a testimony to the greater Rock, and greater object to which we all should stretch the borders of our imagination. Maybe had the prophet Isaiah been here on this beach he would have been reminded of his own words: 'Trust in the Lord for ever, for the Lord, the Lord, is the Rock of Ages. And You will keep in perfect peace the one whose mind is steadfast, because he trusts in You.' Isaiah 26.3,4.

Stretching the borders of our safety

And the cow jumped over …. the fence. Or the cow almost jumped over the fence, and it was a good job Pete was walking past to see it, as he wandered down the lane to see how much the river had overflowed the road. Last week there had been a floating car, the day the rains came, and they had crept over the boot room floor and started to come into the house. Other friends told harder stories of the deluge.

Yesterday morning was not so bad, except for the cow who tried to jump the fence. He was a steer who had wandered as a stranger into the farm a while ago, and was running with the herd on the farm. He was used to running free. He was young and impetuous and suffered from sight in only one eye. The day before, we had moved the herd from the field by the lane into the rough pasture of the ball, but he in his nervousness hadn't followed. We left him in the field on his own and called the owner to collect the next day. That should be easier on his own, except that he wanted to jumped the fence.

He wanted to jump the fence because he saw and heard the others across the wall grazing on some fresh pasture. The jump itself might have challenged a lively jump horse. He, however, was a game or foolish spirit, and tried to jump, or sort of lollop, over the barbed wire fence, which he sort of did, except that he caught his foot in the fence; and each wriggle and wrench only served to make it worse, and tire him out. By the time I came over to help Pete, he was exhausted and frightened. We tried what we could, but to no avail.

We phoned John the farmer, who came over with an iron bar, and with care and leverage and strength between us managed to release him. Now he was stuck between a wire fence and stone wall. He chose to attempt the highest part of the wall, but got stuck on the top, weary with fighting. A prod and a shove, and he was over. But there was another fence, and he got stuck in that. His life had in a few minutes become a series of entrapments. Now it was our turn to clamber through the fence and onto the wall, and fortunately eased him free. Free at last. With a shake of the head, a sound of relief, all perhaps with a thank you, he trotted away to find the herd.

Later we learned he was happy back among his adopted family.

Not unlike that steer, we fall in from one mess to another, and our search for solutions only seems to make matters worse. Thank God for helpers, armed with patience, or strong words, or sympathy, or wisdom, or some combination of all of them.

Isaiah the prophet spoke his message to folk like us who get in a tangle: 'Though grace is shown, they do not learn righteousness. Although, O Lord, your hand is lifted high, they do not see it.' O Lord, protect me from that poor sightedness, where I turn a blind eye to your help, to your grace.

'Yes, Lord, walking in the ways of your judgments, we wait for you. Your name and your renown are the desire of our hearts.' Isaiah 26.8,10,11.

O Lord, give me that true eye to follow your paths – day by day.

Stretching the borders

We said the aim was to stretch their borders. To stretch the borders of their experience, of their imagination, of their persistence. To stretch the borders of their lives. I think without doubt there was a bit of a stretch.

As they walked from Haytor, curtained by the mist, down into the quarry, where people were wild swimming, with half a thought about the quarrymen of two centuries ago, and the granite railway, hand carved, pulled by ponies, which we followed along the moor, the boys in and out of the bracken and gorse, pausing to pull at blackberries. And followed it down and down, where at times it was half a track, or no track, or just an occasional track. Down and down, with barely a murmur, until we reached Yarner Woods, where Albert the woodman met us and introduced us to the forest and something of its life.

As they walked in wind and rain. Or worked around the animals in wind and rain, all togged up. Or walked at night as dusk settled, and the wind whistled and whined across the valley, and shook the trees, and sent the soft warm upland rain whirling and swirling and wetting every face, and blowing off hats or hoods.

As they joined with farmer John to move the pigs. Not as simple as it sounds. Two pregnant sows, from the field behind the house, up around the wall and bank, through the field of sheep, that the sheep dog was itching to round up if only he was allowed; past where the black cow stood, with her three day old calf, quietly nestling against the grey granite wall. All the boys joined in with glee and varying degrees of effort. Trust me it is not the easiest thing to lead a pig, with poor sight, with a will of her own, and following her, nose close to the ground. That job done, they had to assist with guiding another sow from the animal barn out to the field to join the boar and three other sows. That was the easy part. The next part was when the trouble started, and the other sows wanted to row with the newcomer. There was a bit of a fight and shoving against the fences. We left them to sort out their pecking order.

There is no doubt that we helped to stretch their borders. That we opened their inner city eyes and touch and smells and maybe thinking. On the way home, after a last drive through the village, we gave the boys back their phones and electronic devices, and within minutes they were glued to their screens. So were they retreating behind their borders, or had we stretched the borders just a bit, for a while, stored into their memories like data, to which these lads will return with eagerness?

I suspect it is no different for us. There is a similar ambivalence, the stretching and the drawing back, the widening of horizons and closing of the curtains. Isaiah the prophet described a similar thought: 'Lord, you establish peace for us. All that we have accomplished you have done for us.' Isaiah 26.12. We live in a balance of our doing and God's providing, of our efforts and God's accomplishing grace.

A prayer: 'Lord, order a peaceful and whole life for us, because everything we've done, you've done for us.' (The Message Bible).

One more stretch

There are four towering chestnut trees on the village green. Already the sharp green shells are falling on the grass, soon to split apart to show the shiny brown conker. It is a fetching village sight. The chestnut trees bordering the grass. The moor ponies who come to graze or beg something tasty from tourists. The towering church, the cathedral in the moor, with its four clocks facing all four compass points. The row of granite houses that double as souvenir shops. The hut by the field car park that sells ice cream, plus a dollop of Devon cream for the connoisseur.

You first see the village all of a sudden, as the road from Haytor dips sharply, and descends twenty degrees down towards the valley floor, Widecombe, the valley of the withers. First the steepness of the valley, and the fields spreading up the farther side, then the tower of the church, and the cemetery before it, with the gravestones of many local names, including those of Rosemary and Elizabeth of Providence and Shallowford fame. Down past high sided hedges, carefully past the grazing sheep, across the quiet flowing East Webburn river, and up a short rise to the village green, and to the four chestnuts.

Only there are only three and a bit now, because one had to come down during Covid-19. One too many storms had shaken and cracked its swaying boughs. I would like to have been there the day they closed the roads, and bough by bough they dismantled the old thing. In its day a steel bench ran round it and countless families have sat and sucked their ice creams. Perhaps ten children could have linked arms around it. They will restore the bench around the stump, and a fine stump it is. About eight feet high it stands shorn of its beauty, but maybe it will sprout, and its irrepressible life source will find a way for some kind of renewal.

I reckon that Isaiah the prophet watched the woodman working on a tree or two. Only he saw something different. Indeed he envisaged something special. He observed how something so final as a towering tree cut down to its stump, can revive and grow again, albeit into a different shape, and grow and flower and fruit, and out of what seemed dead and over is renewed to new life. The cut down tree supplied him with a picture of hope, of hope in Christ.

'A shoot will come up from the stump of Jesse. From his roots a Branch will bear fruit. The Spirit of the Lord will rest upon him – the Spirit of wisdom and understanding, the Spirit of counsel and of power, the Spirit of knowledge and of the fear of the Lord – and he will delight in the fear of the Lord.' Isaiah 11.1-3.

We have thought about stretching the borders of our imagination, our experience, our perseverance, our lives. This is the one stretch we need to make sure we address. To find the renewal that comes to our lives through encounter with Christ. There is no doubt that that is where true life renewal is found. To our loss we miss it, because we have not stretched that far. To our gain we find it, or he finds us.

There are four chestnut trees on the village green. I will keep my eyes on the fourth one, the stump, to see if it renews, to see if the life will show itself.

Chapter 8: A Beautiful Day in the Neighbourhood

One Day in September

It is a good start to the day. The sun is up, the breeze is up, the clouds are lifting – it will be a beautiful day in the neighbourhood.

The foxes have started to sleep on the soft top of a neighbour's car. The neighbour is not sure if it is a good thing or not. They wail and squeal a bit at night. She is not sure if they are in love or voicing some dispute. Personally, I blame them for the broken milk bottle outside our front door.

I was finishing off something in my study, when I noticed a man on a bicycle stop outside one of the houses opposite. He had a club hammer in his hand, and started to hit the windows of the car parked outside. That was not so easy, so he started on the front windows of the house, which gave way with a crash. I opened my study window and yelled at him, but he seemed not to respond to 'Oy!' As the householder came out of his front door, I called the police and reported what I saw as it happened. Only not much happened. After an exchange of abuse the man with the hammer got on his bike and rode off. The householder went back in and came out with a long crow bar, while his wife stood at the door in her nightie. Their immediate neighbour was out by now and also phoning the police. I was on my way out of the house, and went over and shared a word. Someone somewhere has clearly upset someone.

A house nearby was burgled. Unlocked porch door opened, smashed the glass of the inner door, and in to search the premises. A neighbour has installed a new alarm system. They appear to have more cameras than they have doors, with any intrusion relayed to their smart phone. Another neighbour is moving – a fresh start they say. Another family will come in to put down roots, find a place within the community, become neighbours.

It's a beautiful day in the neighbourhood.

A prayer for living in the neighbourhood: 'Do good to your servant according to your word, O Lord.' Psalm 119.65.

Day Two

Here is a quotation to disturb a beautiful day in the neighbourhood: 'If we want to enjoy the precious relevance of Jesus in our day-to-day, we need the truth about death into our day-to-day. Death-awareness is our path into liberating, life giving truth about Jesus.' That was Pastor Matt McCullough, from Nashville, in an article entitled 'Pornography of death'. He was saying it was a discussion we need to have rather than avoid to have.

I couldn't avoid the subject yesterday. I presided over a funeral. The beautiful thing about a funeral is that it can combine loss and gain, fear and hope. That it brings out love in its different expressions – tears and joy, emotion held in, emotion let out. That it brings out memories and smiles, that it covers over a multitude of sins, and hopefully hides at least for a while the things that don't want to be remembered, or perhaps lays to one side difficult decisions. That it brings people together, and when it is a good funeral, it brings people together well, around a common relationship, a common feeling, a common loss. Yesterday was a good funeral, and a beautiful thing in the neighbourhood.

I spoke with a woman who expressed her love of thirty years for her man. I spoke with a man who was currently unable to speak with his woman after ten years together. I spoke with two fine men who as children it had seemed uncertain what would happen to them in the turmoil of a family turned upside down. I spoke with a man who expressed gratitude for support given and a woman who is making the best of a difficult situation. I spoke with a grieving woman who said that in her loss she will find freedom, and with a woman who says that she has crossed a line in faith and is determined to go forwards and not backwards. I watched children play and grown men cry. I watched women embrace and young men smile and smoke. All trying to be suitably socially distant. It was a beautiful day in the neighbourhood.

It was a day when to face death was to face life. That at least is the idea. Tommy Dorsey lost his wife Nettie in childbirth and their infant son, and his grief was hard to bear. In the service we listened to his song: "Precious Lord, take my hand. Lead me on let me stand. I am tired. I am weak. I am worn. Through the storm, through the night, lead me on to the light. Take my hand, precious Lord, lead me home." These words were also said in the service: 'Being born, being alive, surviving, flourishing, and dying is about putting our hands in the hands of God.' That too is a beautiful thing in the neighbourhood.

The writer of Psalm 119 said, 'Before I was afflicted I went astray, but now I obey your word.' It is all part of the tapestry – the affliction, the straying, the obedience, the trust. The question that sticks in the throat and doesn't always get out is what is the life learning from this? How do I move on in this? Do I move on in this? We don't know what the Psalmist's story was, what knocked him back, what brought him back to his senses. What we do know is that he found 'good knocks' in the 'hard knocks'. 'Before I was brought low I was straying, and now I am determined to keep your word.' Psalm 119.67. (A.Motyer translation).

All these words echo the prayer of another loss bearer who was also a hope carrier: "In life, in death, O Lord, abide with me."

Day Three

I observed two men across the road from Providence. Their car was parked outside the undertakers. Both were sporting dreadlocks. As one man slowly got out of the driver's side, the other stood and talked, animated, waving his hands. The two of them walked towards the little supermarket shop, one more slowly than the other with a limp. I recognised the one with the limp. He used to be in the reggae sound system business, and used to be a champion at table football. A curious connection. At the door of the shop the manager stood to bar their way. There was anger, more waving of hands, doubtless choice language. The shop manager was conceding nothing. The two men were not prepared to take more drastic action. Having said their piece, the one limped back towards the car, and the other strutted voicing his rage, until they drove off, doubtless listening to some dreadlocks music from the car stereo. Another beautiful day in the neighbourhood.

I went into the café next door to the supermarket at some later point and ordered two coffees. I turned and saw a man in his thirties eating a hearty breakfast. A neat full beard, shaved head and bright eyes. We recognised each other and talked. He asked about Providence, and told me of his new job working with young people in the east end of London. He has an interesting name, a name with a message – As One (Asone). We could do with a bit more of that, as one, togetherness. That is always a beautiful thing for the neighbourhood.

I watched as two policemen walked across the road and towards Providence car park. They saw me and gestured. I had not seen either to talk to for a while, though I had seen them go about their business in the neighbourhood. Today they were going to sort out some complaints. There had been complaints from residents, and from pedestrians walking along the passage from the station that passes by Providence. There has been an expansion in drinking on the street after hours, added to by a bit of music, added to allegedly by certain transactions taking place. This is a no drinking on the street zone. We talked about it. We talked about the area. They were going to have a word in the first instance. We want people to be able to get on. That is a beautiful thing for the neighbourhood.

'Lord, teach me good discretion and knowledge, for I believe in your commandments.' Psalm 119.66. (A.Motyer translation).

Good discretion is a good thing. It is a good thing for the neighbourhood. The shop keeper needed it. The police need it. I need it. I need it in the work we do. We need it in the work we do. You need it. We need it as a gift from God. We need it as something that grows from our experience with and engagement with the Word of God. With his commandments. 'Lord, I believe in your commands: teach me knowledge and good judgment.'

On the way home as I drove slowly down my street, I saw the fox, sitting watching by the side of the road. I slowed down and opened my window and looked at him. He looked at me. I think he thought I was neighbourhood watch, so he slunk away, dragging his auburn tail behind. It has been a beautiful day in the neighbourhood.

Day Four

I saw a demonstration of power in the neighbourhood. There was an adult male, fully grown, magnificent, and his great antlers making him seem even bigger than he was. He was with his herd of females and young deer at Richmond Park, not far from the Isabella Plantation. It was a dry broad stretch of grassland, and an intruder came, clearly a younger male, part of the new generation. He was chancing his luck. The great stag came out towards him to stare him out, making himself as big as he could. He circled towards him. There were moments of just standing, the pair of them, thirty yards apart. Then the older stag lifted his nose high, his antlers shaking, and bellowed. The upstart stag got the message, dropped his head, his smaller set of antlers almost pointing to the ground, and sauntered off. Another time perhaps. Another year. At the roar of the stag a group of hinds, who had been grazing apart from the herd, came scampering past the stern glare of their impressive leader. That was an interesting day in the neighbourhood.

I saw something that at first looked weak and tenuous in the neighbourhood. But I was wrong. It was tough, and wiry, and made the most of very little. It was like a metaphor of holding on, of making something out of nothing, of doing good in the neighbourhood. Our back yard is a bit of a mess. A pile of dried out cuttings, some odds and ends of metal objects, and old plastic containers, waiting for a trip to the dump. A touch of soil where long ago we probably tried to grow something unsuccessfully. A stretch of concrete by the shed, leading to the back fence and a back, door-size gate that leads to an alley between the gardens in the neighbourhood. An evening primrose has grown there, out a crack in the concrete, and has grown to four feet, and spread itself out. Its bright yellow flowers like lights at the bottom of the garden. It is a beautiful thing in the neighbourhood.

It doesn't require a demonstration of power to be strong. It requires an opening, just a crack to plant. Just an opportunity and a tenacity, a doggedness, a seeding of faith, a watering of courage. A willingness to follow the light of Christ. He does the rest. He who is good and is ever doing good. To lean after him as the primrose leans after the light. All this is a beautiful thing in the neighbourhood.

A good thought for the neighbourhood: 'You are good, O Lord, and what you do is good. Teach me your ways.' Psalm 119.68.

Day Five

She came again to the door of Providence with that look, repeating her previous chorus of I cannot cope and I have lost everything. We had children soon to come in, so for safeguarding reasons we couldn't let her in. We put a chair and table outside and gave her a hot meal, and cup of tea and banoffee pie. We made it clear that today was not a day she could come in. A short while later I walked down the road to a meeting, and on passing the pharmacist saw a policeman escort her out, and usher her back up the road. She wandered back up towards our end of the street and entered the Red Cross shop and lay on the floor whimpering. I later heard that police had to be called to quietly escort back towards her flat. Another day I attended a meeting about her with professionals concerning her case and circumstances.

I attended a meeting in a community hall. The subject matter was quite serious. There were arguments and raised voices, anger and walk out, and some uncertainty as how to proceed.

He called at the window for a reference and said he had suffered wrongful dismissal. He called at the window to say his prostate is improving and doesn't need to return for six months. He stopped by to say that he is about to take his very elderly mother for probably one more trip to the land of her birth. He is nervous, but we wish it goes really well.

In a church I saw Jesus on the cross, Christ crucified, standing above the rood screen, with two wooden figures gazing at him, as faithful have ever gazed. Christ crucified hanging on the cross, a reminder in this church each week, of all our weaknesses, of all his grace. I saw Christ on the cross and saw that he had come for helpless ones, all out of sorts with everyday life. I saw Christ on the cross and recalled that he had died for angry ones, for whom the world is out of focus, skewed. I saw him on the cross, and knew he had come for me, and died, and risen, and coming again.

I thought about redemption for the neighbourhood.

'My soul faints with longing for your salvation, but I have put my hope in your word.' Psalm 119.81.

Chapter 9: Talk about Heroes

Not for me, but for us

October. He is getting his statue at last. I read it in the local paper. At a time when people have been pulling down statues, although that momentum seems to have eased, he is getting one. He has already had two schools named after him in Wandsworth, one a secondary school that many Providence boys attended, now long since closed, and the other a local primary not so long ago named after him.

A few weeks before the leader of Wandsworth Council announced funding for a new statue of John Archer, past Mayor of Battersea, and London's first black Mayor. He said "Now seems the right time to look for positive role models and to celebrate the achievements of John Archer who remains an inspiration for so many people." Amen to that! We are certainly on the lookout for positive role models.

As is well known, John Archer, the son of a merchant seaman from Barbados and an Irish woman, was born in Liverpool, not Battersea in 1863. Having himself travelled a fair bit around the world, he came to Battersea in his late twenties with his black Canadian wife Bertha, and set himself up as a photographer along Battersea Park Road. Drawn into local politics he was elected as councillor for Latchmere, which is the ward that still serves Providence House, and was elected as Mayor of Battersea in 1913.

In his speech that night he declared, "For the first time in the history of the English nation a man of colour has been elected as mayor of an English borough. That will go forth to the coloured nations of the world and they will look to Battersea and say Battersea has done many things in the past, but the greatest thing it has done has been to show that it has no racial prejudice and that it recognises a man for the work he has done."

That is a good thought that people should look to Battersea as a model of racial integration, but I don't really think we can. John Archer also said that the hardest thing about being Mayor was not being in the chair, but being looked at as 'a man of colour.' Hopefully in that sense things have changed since then.

The leader of the Council in his speech announcing the memorial statue said that "There is a motto attributed to Battersea that reads 'Not for me, not for thee, but for us'. And this seems more fitting than ever to help raise a public statue for this famous son of Battersea.' I am not quite sure where the motto comes from, but it certainly has a resonance: not for me, not for you, but for us.

We would all do well to take that on board. Or in the words of that famous prayer: "Teach me good Lord to serve thee as thou deservest, to give and not to count the cost, to fight and not to heed the wounds, to toil and not to seek for rest, to labour and not to ask for any reward, save that of knowing that we do thy will." (Ignatius Loyola).

A Speck of Dust

There are no statues to him, nor a blue plaque to say he lived here. There is a still a sign in the seaside town pointing the way to the Museum that bears his name, although the Museum is no longer there, but lives virtually in the ether, or stored in boxes in a loft.

He was a painter and poet, a preacher and politician, a writer and thinker, a researcher and collector, a broadcaster and story teller, and a bit of an inventor. He was a father of six and it was as father that he taught me something vital that has accompanied all my life. He was not a black man, but he taught me from knee height the principle of acceptance and of different peoples being together. Maybe I learned it from his years in Guyana, although I have no memories of my birthplace in Georgetown, no memory of beginning to grow up among children of different backgrounds and colour. I have a vivid early memory of the large oval dining table in the house in Croydon around which all twenty one seats, apart from family, were filled with Guyanese people. I have no idea who they were or how much since my father kept in touch. But it was there from the beginning – something about acceptance.

Having spent my whole working life among the Caribbean community in Battersea and at Providence, and especially from the seventies onwards, feeling I was part of something, and seeming to have little problem seamlessly fitting it, I have at times wondered why it worked out. It was there from the beginning – something about acceptance. It worked both ways and it has always made a difference. It was often said – white but black inside. I owe it to my father for a good beginning.

I owe two other things to my father. First that he brought us up in a household of Christian faith. It is almost like he put all the components around us, and sort of left it for us to piece together. Church, Sunday School, his preaching, books, the Bible, grace at meals – always. The principle of service, of giving and frugality, of hospitality, of having and having not. As children we all made our way to faith in different ways. For me it was specific, time and date, of conscious commitment to Christ in the front parlour. A bit like the apostle Paul's words to the young teacher, Timothy: 'of your sincere faith which first lived in your grandmother and in your mother, and now lives in you also.' 2 Timothy 1.5.

The other thing I owe to my father is a love of football, from playing ball in the park, to watching teams, to hearing him talk, to religiously listening to results, to being taken to Selhurst Park to watch the Palace. A small thing you might think, but one of those life enriching interests. On his death bed he joked about not being fit enough to get picked anymore for the team. Sport was always there to start a conversation that might have difficulty getting it going. Another verse from Paul to Timothy comes to mind, 'that physical training is good, but godliness has value for all things, holding promise for both the present life and the life to come.' 1 Timothy 4.8

He would have been 105 had he lived to this pandemic. He stopped just short of his century by three years, and 95 years past his own father's death in war. In his eighties he painted a large autobiographical picture, a wide range of cameos from different parts of his life. He called it A Speck of Dust, and said that he was just a speck of dust in the history of mankind, but that even something as unnoticed as a speck can makes its mark. That pretty well was the theme of his museum.

I am reminded of a line from the Psalms again, from Psalm 126. There is a picture of a farmer walking out to his ploughed fields, slowly, painstakingly trailing a line of seed across the field, and back and back again, and all in the hope of something better, some great outcome: 'He who goes out weeping, carrying seed to sow, will return with seeds of joy, carrying their sheaves with him.' Psalm 126.6.

To quote my father, 'If we can encourage some, inspire a few and help to lighten another's burden as we pass along that way, our journey will be a happy one.'

Young gifted and black

Walter is a footballer. You could also, with the old song, say that he is young, gifted and black. You could also say he is a Providence boy, from around six years old, when he first tumbled through the youth club doors with his brother. He played football in Chelsea's academy until he was eighteen, when they let him go, after which he became a bit of a sporting nomad, playing professional league football in Greece, Sweden and Portugal, and for a while in English clubs trying to find a place to fit. In 2020 he was parading his skills in Derry City. The last time I saw him he was making a promotional film about his career, and filmed some of it in Providence House. The last time we communicated, he thanked me for helping his brother out of a bit of trouble.

Walter, another Walter, was a footballer. He was also young gifted and black, but lived in very different times. He died not much older than the other Walter is now. Like John Archer, his father was from Barbados. Born in Folkestone of a Kentish mother, from quite a young age he and his brother were orphaned to a Methodist Home in London. His brother was adopted by a Scottish family and went on to be a dentist, but Walter was to make his mark in football. His sporting journey went from Clapton to Tottenham Hotspurs to Northampton FC, where he played the majority of his professional games, and he had signed for Glasgow Rangers when war broke out.

He was one of the first people of mixed heritage to play in the English football league, and also one of the first black officers in the British army, being promoted to second lieutenant in 1917. He served at the Battle of the Somme, and with commendation in the Italian front, but died in battle in France during the German Spring Offensive of 1918. His body was never recovered, and so joined that mournful multitude of men lost out of season.

Of his football it was written of him after a match for Spurs, that "Tull was the best forward on the field. So clean in mind and method as to be a model for all white men who play football" It was also the game in which the racial abuse towards him was so unremitting, that Spurs became less eager to pick him after that.

Of his character and career, it was engraved in a memorial at the Northampton FC stadium: "Through his actions, W. D. J. Tull ridiculed the barriers of ignorance that tried to deny people of colour equality with their contemporaries. His life stands testament to a determination to confront those people and those obstacles that sought to diminish him and the world in which he lived. It reveals a man, though rendered breathless in his prime, whose strong heart still beats loudly."

He has no statue. That apparently was a problem with the legal process of military statue making, but he has a blue plaque where he lived in London as a child, a road named after him in Northampton and a pub named after him, if it is still open during these difficult days.

If we are looking for a model for inspiration we could stay with Walter: "a determination to confront … those obstacles that sought to diminish him in the world." There are always obstacles to diminish us in this world. It almost seems at times that it is the purpose of public speaking to take away from someone else. We too can fall into that same mindset of diminishing. It is time we developed a culture of affirmation.

A verse from Scripture comes to mind – of course. From chapter 11 of the Letter to the Hebrews, where the writer has indulged his imagination with his own culture of affirmation about heroes of the faith. He ends by saying something that in the first instance seems sad: 'The world was not worthy of them.' What an awful thing to be said of us, were it to be said, that we are not worthy of them, of Walter Tull, of others, because we diminished them, we dismissed them as not being much, when all along it is we who are the less, not them.

The next sentence is written for our inspiration, that we might be those with a determination to confront those obstacles that sought to diminish in this world: 'These were all commended for their faith, yet none of them received what had been promised. God had planned something better for us so that only together with us would they be made perfect.' Hebrews 11.38-40.

As it says in another place: the just shall live by faith (Habakkuk

2.4). Meanwhile I think I will message the other Walter and see how he is getting on.

Finding a place

I suppose today you would say she was Middle-Eastern, Jordanian even. I suppose you would say she was a refugee, about which we have a lot to say today. In her time there was a wonderful phrase – sojourner, about which in her day there was also a lot to say. It has a ring of travelling, staying and moving on, here for a while, not forever. Possibly looking to settle somewhere. The irony of her story is she met and married a refugee in her own land, but later herself became a refugee in his land. I suspect that today there are similar stories.

Back to the beginning: her family got to know an immigrant family. We would call them economic migrants today, because it was famine that had driven them from their homeland. It was a reluctant departure, but they felt it necessary for survival. They had hung on too long. To their land of adoption they had travelled on foot, and there is a lot of walking in the migrant life. Today we might have called them a nuclear family, husband, wife, two kids, boys in fact. As migrant boys might well do, they took a fancy to a couple of local girls, and they were married. We don't know if it was for love, for convenience, for better citizenship prospects, or a plain good deal. Either way two migrant lads married two local girls and a mixed race family was formed.

Unfortunately, seeking a better life abroad doesn't guarantee that it all goes well. At first there were good signs. A comfortable life, and two marriages, but sometimes trouble follows like a stalker, something we are getting nervously close to in our day. First, the old man died, and that was sad because in his heart he really wanted to return to the homeland. Then one by one the husbands died, leaving three widows, and no children. It created a crisis in more ways than one.

At first the plan was that all three women should stay together, and gain strength in numbers and comfort together in sorrow, and maybe become economic migrants together and make their way back to the mother-in-law's homeland, because word had it that things had improved. That was the first plan, but one of the widowed daughters-in-law had second thoughts, and the prospect of travelling to an unknown country on a bit of chance was too much. She elected to stay put and try and find a life among her own people.

The other daughter-in-law was made of sterner stuff, or more adventurous stuff, or perhaps she was one of those people who make a commitment before God and keep it. Probably too she felt for the mental health of her mother-in-law, who at the best of times was poor company, but right now was darn hard to live with. She had stopped calling herself by her own name, a pretty name, Naomi, which means pleasant, but it seemed that every time she heard her name called it reminded her how unpleasant life had become. So when people greeted her, she began to reply don't call me Naomi, call me Mara, which means bitter. Bitter because life had dealt her a deck of stained cards – nationless, husbandless, childless, friendless, and even Godless. That is how she felt.

Her daughter-in-law despite all this was drawn to her. Or perhaps because of all this she was drawn deeper to her, because as they say a friend in need is a friend indeed, and this friend was without doubt in need. So she ignored Naomi-Mara's plea to stay put. While Naomi made her hesitant, grieving way back to the land of her birth, still wearing the mourning colours of black, she declared she would stay by Naomi-Mara through thick and thin.

In fact this is what she famously said, and it is of such a high quality that women and men have taken it as an example of what commitment means. We live in a day of promises not kept, of starting things and not finishing, of beginnings without end. Not so this woman, who said to her mother-in-law: 'Where you go I will go. Where you stay I will stay. Your people will be my people and your God my God. Where you die I will die, and there I will be buried. May the Lord deal with me, be it ever so severely, if anything but death separates you and me.'

So the sojourner returned home, and the homegirl became a migrant. And Mara grew out of her bitterness and, when pleasanter times returned, took back the name of Naomi. Home was the little town of Bethlehem and that became home too for Ruth, for that was her name if you haven't yet guessed it. Life was hard at first, and both scraped a living with many times a hungry belly, but Ruth's commitment was noticed, and in the end she was married to an older, richer, man, and their lives were made as secure as it can be in a transient world. Her story is told in the Old Testament book of Ruth.

We all love a bit of genealogy, and theirs is recorded too: 'Boaz married Ruth and he was the father of Obed, the father of Jesse, and Jesse the father of King David.' Then following forwards through fourteen generations, we read that a certain 'Jacob was the father of Joseph, the husband of Mary, of whom was born Jesus, who is called the Christ.' All of which is recorded in Matthew chapter 1.

There is a whole thread of migration and sojourning, of twists and turns, of unexpected junctures in the story of grace in the Bible; just as there is repeated storytelling of those who made their choices on principle, on commitment, out of loyalty to need and kindness, out of trust in God, even trust in God when they knew so little of him, but when they knew enough to say: 'Your God will be my God.'

Like Ruth let us choose well when life is bitter and when life is pleasant.

Talk about heroes

Lockdown has probably given some people too much time on their hands. Too much time to pour over the lives of those who once were heroes, but now whose past gets stained with the present. Lockdown has probably given some people too little time on their hands. Too little time to recognise the hero inside of some others of us. Perhaps Captain Tom has done us a favour.

For ninety-nine years he was known to those who knew him as an ordinary man, a good man, a respected man, a loved man. Even the exploit that brought him fame started as the act of a committed, brave, dedicated ordinary man, doing his bit in walking around his own bit of land. Now he will be remembered for the 38 million pounds or more that he raised for the NHS, a hero of the pandemic, and accolades he received so late in life. Is it that he is like one of us, and not part of the professionalised fame industry that we warmed so much to him.

The apostle Paul wrote to some ordinary Christian people, in his letter to the Colossians: 'Whatever you do, work at it with all your heart.' Colossians 3.23. I think Captain Tom would have echoed that. The apostle adds an extra motive: 'as working for the Lord, not for men. It is the Lord you are serving.' It is a maxim for ordinary people to work at what you do with all your heart. It is a deeper maxim to work in what you do with all your heart, as working for the Lord.

We need heroes. We need to know that ordinary people can be heroes. We need to know that what we do, with all our hearts, can count for something, and better can count for something with God. Back to John Archer, 'Not for me, not for thee, but for us.' We could do with some more of that.

Chapter 10: Coming Storm

Walk on by. November

He sat apart. Very much apart. In fact none of the others were to be seen. It was almost as if he sat there to be looked at, because that is what others did. They passed by and looked at him, and made the remark that he was there all alone. Some even took pictures of him. We ourselves actually made a detour to look at him, and went relatively close, but not close enough for a conversation. We did take photographs though. Clearly in his prime he had been quite a guy, without doubt a leader of others. Now all that was past and he was left to ruminate on his own. Forgotten and left to his own ways, possibly his own destiny.

We saw him because we were with a gaggle of noisy children in Richmond Park. We had promised them deer, but he was the only one we saw all afternoon. I can still seem him in my mind. Sat on the wet meadow, partly hidden by the tall spiky grass. It was his great crown of antlers that caught the eye from a couple of hundred yards away. He had to endure the cackle of boys, brave and noisy from thirty yards, and the curiosity of the girls in the group. All talking about him. He had endured worse. Indeed he must have endured worse, probably as recently as this autumn the triumphalist braying of some younger stag that had usurped his position as leader of the herd. Were he a man he would have reflected on the fragility of positions in society, of the perils of leadership and the short fixed fidelity of those he had thought had been with him, as 'false as water' as the bard says. I wonder what he did think about, as he faced a hard winter ahead, forgotten. We walked on to the see the geese and swans on Pen Pond. He kept staring in the grey sky and chewed the cud.

According to Kay Morgan-Gurr the largest group in the world unreached by Christian ministry is 'those with disabilities and additional needs. They face huge amounts of injustice in every area of their lives and have done so for centuries. The church doesn't seem interested.' Forgotten?

Last night I had a phone conversation with a woman with additional needs. She was on my mind because she had been texting me and I had not responded. She spoke almost without pause for fifteen minutes, about her situation, about Covid, about living alone, about being with people, about an operation she is to have, about recurring memories of the tragic association that impacted her life and still does. It was good to have spoken, and it made me more comfortable that she wasn't in an impossible place. Yet still by putting down the phone there is a sense in which I am walking on and leaving her to remain in her place chewing the cud as it were. Forgotten? Hopefully not.

These stories can be repeated, of people struggling in their needs, of friends and associates walking on by, and of far worse as the news reports almost daily remind us. This next quotation is not a platitude, nor a piece of performance piety. It is the strength that is carved out of faith. It is the focus of the forgotten, whose faith firmly rests in the Father. It is that place of trust to know, that even if others walk on, He doesn't walk on by.

'Though my father and mother forsake me, the Lord will receive me. Teach me your way, O Lord, lead me in a straight path, despite the efforts of those who work against me. Wait for the Lord. Be strong and take heart, and wait for the Lord.' Psalm 27.10

The reason to wait, and to wait in hope, is because He will not walk on by.

Drifting eyes

It was in the eyes I think. It was always in the eyes I think. That movement of gaze that connected to uncertainty. There had always been that uncertainty as far as I could remember. That hesitancy about where I belong, where I fit in, what I am part of, and wanting to belong, wanting to fit in, to be a part of. I suppose it could be said that what we provided, or didn't provide, when he came regularly to us, didn't help him find that place, his place. Or perhaps it diverted him from something worse. 'Part of our lives' had been our strapline. Perhaps it wasn't enough.

He is back coming to us. Possibly. For a while. He has been coming to attend an online course that will prepare him for work readiness. He appears to have been enjoying it. I chatted with him one day. I asked where he hoped it might all lead. He reminded me that he was still getting his feet on the ground after a period in prison. He reminded me that the charge had been for 'intent to supply'. I asked him if he still intended to supply and there was that look again. The uncertain look, that swaying in the wind. That look of I might be going this way or I might be going that way; but what was sure is that I am not sure which way I am going. We spoke about how this course and other things needed to lead him to a better path, because the other way is the road to nowhere. To misquote Jesus: and many walk along it. (Matthew 7.13).

Last week there was a row. Something went missing and the finger seemed to logically point to him. He was there, he had opportunity, he had form. Ah, that old chestnut – he had form! I think his whole life has been a catalogue of those situations, from home, to school, to street. Another reason for the drifting eyes. Caught in a corner, which way to go? In the end it was alright – sort of, but he didn't come last week. Although he said he would on the day of the next appointment. Is that because he was angry, or because he was in fact guilty, or because he was on the way and he met a better offer and went along with them? Either way there would have been that drifting in his gaze.

I am praying he will keep coming. I am praying that we will speak with him. I am praying that he will find a new focus, a settled gaze, a steady eye. I am thinking of this verse for him from Psalm 148.14: 'Let us praise the name of the Lord. He has raised up strength for his people, the praise of all his saints, the people close to his heart.' I pray for him to discover that he is close to the heart of God. For that is where belonging is.

Prayer for today. You pray and you think of someone close to you who needs that re-focus, that re-connection, that homing instinct, that sense that they are close to the heart of God.

Out of reach

There is nothing more that she wants, and really she should have it. It is what a mother should have, or in her case a grandmother should have. But she can't. Something has happened that is beyond her reach to do much about. It is not that she hasn't tried. She is afraid that the more she tries the worse it might get. There had been a breakdown in relationships. Not hers as such. Not of her doing. But now it affects her. It affects her on the inside and on the outside, and she can no longer see the little ones she longs to see. It is like she has been cut off, prevented. The door has been shut. She asked the other day whether she should actually go and knock on that door, but we counselled her not to.

She walks a lot. In part I suspect she walks to walk off the pain. Each time we meet her we talk about it. We tell her that we are praying. And we do. We pray that she would have the patience of faith, that waiting in hope for the corner to turn, for things to settle, for things to change. There is such a thing as the patience of faith: 'I waited patiently for the Lord. He turned to me and heard my cry.' Psalm 40.1. The waiting is hard enough, but the patiently is harder still. We pray that she would have the patience of faith, and to look for those little answers, those small signs of change.

She is not the only family we know with troubles. Another that is worked closely with at Providence House. A mother and daughter where the simmering, unresolved concerns exploded into a fight last weekend, and the one is in temporary care, getting what she wanted, but not getting what she really wanted or what she needs, and the other nursing bewilderment, and other emotions, and probably not seeing something she should.

What we all know is that none of these relationships are as they should be. Lord, keep me from words that poison relationships. Keep me from attitudes that build a wall between us. Lord, keep me from that unseeing that doesn't notice we are drifting, drifting away, drifting apart, and then drifting out of reach.

I am thinking again of how God feels in all this. I have enough of a hint in scripture to ask that question. Psalm 148.14: 'Let us praise the name of the Lord. He has raised up strength for his people, the praise of all his saints, the people close to his heart.' I am trusting that these people may be close to the heart of God. So I am praying for them. We are praying for them.

Prayer for today. You pray and you think of someone close to you who needs that joining back together, that healing of connections, indeed that family sense that comes to those drawn close to the heart of God. Maybe you are that person, so pray for yourself. 'Let us praise the name of the Lord. He has raised up strength for his people, the praise of all his saints, the people close to his heart.'

Windswept not blown away

We were swept off our feet. If we had had wings, I think we could have flown. To put it mildly Branscombe cliffs were breezy that day. The Psalmist speaks of the Lord who 'brings out the wind from his storehouses.' Psalm 135.7. I think someone left the door open all that day and night.

The sea was brown with rage and foaming at the mouth, and hissing through its teeth at every breath of the breaking waves, rattling the pebbles, with its hiss echoing all the way along the sand. This stretch of coast has lived through every winter battering for generations, and has its own memory of a weather induced land collapse. Just two hundred years ago several hundred yards of the Hooken cliff edge slipped and crashed below, forming the undercliff along which we tripped and slithered in the flinty mud as we edged our way down to the shore. Three pinnacles of chalk cliff now stand alone, like three white sisters looking out to sea to watch the boats come in, or rather to wait for the next storm.

We saw something intriguing from the windblown cliff top, special even. We watched a kestrel almost stationery in the high wind below the cliff top. So small! Perhaps little more than two hands width, its wings aflurry, and yet as hard as the wind hurled its blast, the little predator held its hover position above the wooded undercliff watching whatever it watched with its telescopic eyes. We could have watched for longer, but we could barely stand, and left it to its genius and to its hunt.

It made me think, though, about resisting the pressures, about standing against the winds of life. There are enough of them about. Lockdown, the spread of the virus, the fear it brings, the restrictions that inconvenience, or wear down, or downright threaten the business. How to see beyond it or to live with it. There are others. The pressure to conform, or to buckle. The pressure against belief, or to loosen the grip of faith. The pressure to lose heart, or to drop standards, and what the heck! We each have our own pressures.

The apostle Paul, of course, writes about the pressure. He says there are more pressures than the obvious ones to contend with. It is bad enough with the troubles we can see that come as flesh and blood, but it's those unexpected ones, those subtle undermining influences that are harder to combat. He writes of 'the powers of this dark world and the spiritual forces of evil.' Ephesians 6.10-18. And he says we have to stand, or take our stand. Like the little kestrel to hold your position in the storm. 'Finally', the apostle says, 'be strong in the Lord and in his mighty power.'

He goes onto to speak about truth bound to us like a belt tightened up, not loosely attached; of righteousness close to our chest, because how we live is who we are and who we are is vital in this task. He writes of faith and peace, and of hope, without which it is hard to weather the storms that come our way. He talks of trusting in the word of God, as a life saver, as a weapon; and above all he writes of prayer – 'on all occasions with all kinds of prayers and requests.'

I don't know what the weather will be like today, whether the wind will be up again driving the rain, or more settled with a hint of sun through the clouds. I suspect the kestrel will be on the hunt again, riding the air waves, holding his helicopter course in the wind. I don't know what it is that we face today, but I know, with Psalm 135, that there is strength in the promises of God.

'I know that the Lord is great. I know that our Lord is greater than all other powers. I know that he makes the choices that pleases him, in the heavens and on the earth, in the seas and in the depths. I know he makes the clouds to rise from the ends of the earth, and he brings out the wind from his storehouses.'

Button up then.

Coming Storm

There is a storm coming. I heard it in the night. I saw it pound the harbour walls, crash and spume and roll in again and again. The grey rolling foaming surge breaking against the Cob and leaping its walls with showers of salty spray. I heard the wind-whistling of the storm and the shaking of the bells upon the boats anchored in the harbour mud, and watched the wagtails whirl and swirl in the whirling swirling winds.

I sometimes think the sea could take away all the anger of the world, and coil it up upon the rolling waves, and let it out with a roar upon a million jangling pebbles on the beach. And vent with its spume all the bitterness and wrath and shouting, until it made itself hoarse, relieved of rage, emptied of envy. Until the wild wind drops and the storm calms and the sun comes out, and light shines yellow once again on Golden Cap, reflecting some kind of peace on Stonebarrow's head, witnesses to all the calm and anger of the bay, and of the world.

There is a different storm descending again on us, indiscriminate of who it chooses to affect, and out of which will draw the frustration and the emptiness, the anger and the loss, the wondering and the courage, the 'rage against the dying of the light.' The hesitation and defiance, the reason and the hope. The faith. Please God the faith. Not empty faith. Not even the putting up the shutters faith, trusting from experience that this will pass. But faith in One who is faithful. But faith that I have a purpose in this, because he has given it me. Faith in Him who calms the storm because he brings a storm. Not just to weather the storm but to have come through it wiser, stronger, humbler.

'Give thanks to God, for good is he: for mercy has he ever. Thanks to the God of all give ye, for his grace faileth never.

'Thanks give the Lord of lords unto: for mercy has he ever. Who only wonders great can do: for his grace faileth never.

'In our low state who on us thought, for he has mercy ever. And from our foes our freedom wrought: for his grace faileth never.

'Who does all flesh with help relieve, for he has mercy ever. Thanks to the God of heaven give: for his grace faileth never.' Psalm 139 from Scottish Psalter.

And his grace faileth never. Remember that one in the storm.

I am not sure where this prayer came from, but I am minded to pray it.

A Prayer

Lord, grant me the strength to be strong, the health to be a healer, the peace to be a peacemaker, and the grace to be a giver.

Lord, grant me the poverty to ask for more, the comfort to be a mourner, the meekness to be an inheritor, and the emptiness to be filled.

Lord, grant me the despair to want a Saviour, the bereftness to want a Father, the weakness to want thy Spirit, the aloneness to seek the Trinity.

Lord, grant me the strength to be strong and the grace to be a giver.

Chapter 11: Christmas Cancelled

The Lights are not going out

In August 1914, on the eve of the First World War, Sir Edward Grey made his famous quote: 'The lamps are going out all over Europe, we shall not see them lit again in our lifetime'. He was speaking in his room in the Foreign Office to his journalist friend, the editor of the Westminster Gazette. Looking out from his window, across St. James' Park, it was dusk and the first of the gas lights along the Mall were being lit. The next day Grey would have to face the Cabinet and to persuade them that the time had now come to declare war on Germany. It wasn't completely true fortunately, but for hundreds of thousands of people the lamps were never lit again. What was completely true unfortunately, was that Europe was never the same again. Having said that, those four years of cataclysm lit the torch of social progress in a number of ways, but in other ways it blew out the candle of faith and of believing hope for so many, with its deadly breath.

In a different context Jesus said something that has a resonance with Grey's sombre words. In John chapter 9, Jesus and his disciples are walking along the streets of Jerusalem, when they come across a man begging. Nothing unusual for us in that for today either. This man however was blind. Jesus' disciples appear to ask the sort of dumb question that we tend to ask, thinking not about the man's condition, but the circumstances that got him to where he is. Almost a bit like us at times wanting a reason not to help.

Jesus, in his customary manner defers the disciples' question, and leads on to a different subject to make them think. 'As long as it is day, we must do the work of him who sent me. Night is coming, when no-one can work.' In other words, today is the day of opportunity, seize it, for tomorrow it may be gone. Right now, there is freedom to share the good news, so share it because that freedom may not last. At the moment you have the strength and sight and clarity of mind to do God's work, or to believe in his Name, so get on with it. What is stopping you? It won't always be so.

Those thoughts speak to our situation and to our day. You could even apply it to Covid-19. Who would have imagined that it would be some pandemic that has restricted the movement of those who would do good, or those who would minister Christ's message? We were caught out. How will we find the best way to work through this pandemic night, to do the will of God?

There is another night that is creeping across the sky. It is the slow moving cloud of doubt in society, the shift against any bias to Christian truth, to given Truth. It is the slow moving cloud of the acceptance that brings that form of godliness without the power of holiness. Before we know it, it will be night. Please God, not a night, when no-one can work, or work the work of God.

In the narrative in John chapter 9, Jesus does two things. First, he makes a statement: 'While I am in the world, I am the Light of the world.' The disciples saw that quite readily, for Christ was exactly like that for them, a light, the light. When some months later he died, it was as if that light had been extinguished, and indeed had gone out for ever; but after the resurrection, they realised more fully that he was their light and their life and indeed the Light of the World.

The second thing that Jesus did, was work the work of God as

God's light. In a curious display, he stooped down, spat on the ground, made some mud with the saliva, put it on the man's eyes, and told him to go and wash in the Pool of Siloam. And he did and he washed and the lights came on for the first time in his life, and he went home seeing, because Jesus had done the work for which God had sent him.

Jesus has been turning the lights on in this dark world for men and women ever since. It is to the darkness of my own perception, that Christ would bring light.

Jesus is the light of the world. He is the light of the world for Advent. He is the light of the world for Lockdown. He is the light of the world for a Covid night. In an earlier incident when light needed to expose the darkness, Jesus said: 'I am the Light of the World. Whoever follows me will never walk in darkness, but will have the light of life.' John 8.12.

Faith on the shelf

"I left my faith in a box on a shelf when no God helped and no person cared." Those are not my words, but the words of someone I know. Or perhaps I used to know, and the intervening years have made connection periodic and spasmodic at best. I had reason to be in touch over a project we used to work together on. That was a generation ago. Perhaps I was one of the many he thought didn't care.

He also went on to say that he finds 'people let you down'. I guess that is an all too common feeling. He said too that "the God figure is a silent one when you need help." I didn't think that was the time to quote from that Footsteps poem, that "when you only saw one set of footprints, it was then I carried you." Nor did I think it was time to quote the laments of the prophets who in their journey with God found his silence the hardest to bear: 'How long,

O Lord, must I cry for help, but you do not listen' was the complaint of Habakkuk, who apparently stood on the watchtower literally to see if an answer from God would come.

I did say, however, that I was glad he had left his faith in a box on the shelf, and urged him to keep it there and not throw it away. One day he might want to take it down again. That is my prayer.

My friend is, of course, not alone in this feeling. Of being let down by people. Of feeling that they are the injured party, that they are the one not understood. Of being let down by God.

Advent is a time for starting again, for thinking again. Maybe lockdown was a time for starting again. Perhaps for re-connecting. For finding again what has been let go of, put to one side. Or left on the shelf. In a box. This Covid-Advent is even more a time to re-think and take stock. Not to wait for something transitory, a bit of Christmas past, a taste for something like it was; but to seek for something that is Covid-proof.

Hosea the prophet urged, with these words, folk who were hurting, losing grasp, or just plain waiting: 'Come, let us return to the Lord. He has torn us to pieces. Yes, but he will heal us. He has injured us. Yes, but he will bind up our wounds.

'After two days he will revive us. On the third day he will restore us, that we may live in his presence.

'Let us acknowledge the Lord. Let us press on to acknowledge him.

'As surely as the sun rises, he will appear. He will come to us like the winter rains, and like the spring rains to water the earth.' Hosea 6.1-3.

As surely, he will come, that we may live in his presence.

This Present Age

This present age – now there's an expression. Or the here and now. The current time.

This present age at Providence House. Yesterday we interviewed and appointed a part time admin assistant. Yesterday the junior dancers were filmed performing their 'You are Special' story. Yesterday we made space for some family counselling in the building. Yesterday some of the young people were cooking at Glass Doors a homeless project. All part of being in this present age.

I watched a man with no shoes walking down Cavendish Road in the rain as I drove in the night. I saw two young men, the worse for wear, and tired of this present age walk under the railway bridge at Clapham Junction carrying sleeping bags. I helped up an older larger man whose foot had caught the edge of the curb by the bus stop. He seemed alright. I ignored the young men and women wearing some branded coats stopping people with their clipboards to engage in conversations people didn't want to listen to and they probably half-heartedly believed in, but they knew the patter and could do it with a smile. All part of this present age.

The restaurants are closed again. The tiers came back: London in Tier Three, Devon in Tier Two, The Scilly Isles in Tier One, not that anyone much can get there. Somewhere else in a Tier Four. The tiers at the football grounds and the theatres are empty. They have been saying it is temporary for long enough. They say this is the present age. Our time. Here and now.

Every country has its own version of this crisis. Meanwhile dictatorship in some parts is spreading like a disease. People taken hostage. People trafficked. Refugees on the move. More refugees on the move. Truth is bandied about like a refugee, taken hostage for political ends. Honesty at high levels trafficked along with deceit. The iceberg is drifting past South Georgia. The climate is changing. All part of this present age. This here and now.

The apostle Paul writing to Titus in the New Testament, and saying this is the age you live in - the present age. His present age not the same as our present age, but the challenges are similar though different. Each present age seems to last too long, to have no end in sight. The apostle wrote this: 'In this present age, while we wait for the blessed hope.' Titus 2.13. That's what the coming of Christ meant: we live in this present age, and we deal with it, but although it is for long enough, it is not for ever. We wait for the blessed hope. That he who came once will come again. There will be no tiers then.

In the words of the prophet who visualised the first coming: 'Comfort, comfort my people, says your God. Speak tenderly to Jerusalem, and proclaim to her that her warfare is ended, her hard service has been completed.' Isaiah 40.1-2.

This present age is not for ever. It is for the present. We wait for the blessed hope. In the present age, we wait for the blessed hope. 'Even so, Lord, come.'

The Reckoning

The day couldn't have started better. It began by my thinking of the Glory of God. It continued at the tyre place where the mechanic assured me that my tyre was fine and no need to change it. At the computer repair shop the kind man said he wouldn't charge for his time only for the part purchased. He was happy to do it. There was a good start to the morning. Happy human contact with cooperative people. I felt positive and passing the lady outside Iceland, who seated on her piece of cardboard, with her arms waving in front of her pleading, with the almost empty cup in her begging hand, I felt generous and thought I would give her what was in my purse. There was only 31 pence, and nothing in my wallet, so my generosity somewhat faded, and I walked onto the car. The rest of the day descended into bureaucracy, trying to finish off end of year 'stuff' at Providence House, and attending a long meeting about 'stuff'. I suppose there is always a reckoning.

The excitement about vaccinations seems to be getting lost amidst the renewed threat to Christmas. A sort of 'Christmas but' is being construed. Celebrate Christmas by all means, but…. but be careful, but don't mix, but be selective in the travel arrangements. The politicians who don't have to make the decisions are being free with their advice to the politicians who do have to make the decisions. The thing about this virus is that there was always going to be a reckoning. With the inevitably of the arrival of a variant strain, it was always likely that little would go to plan.

I suppose it could be said that Christ came because there was going to be a reckoning. Back to Paul's letter to Titus in the New Testament: 'For the grace of God has appeared that offers salvation to all people.' He brought salvation to save us from the reckoning. The apostle goes on: 'It teaches us to say "No" to ungodliness and worldly passions, and to live self-controlled, upright and godly lives in this present age.' That is how we conduct our lives before the day of reckoning. He adds: 'while we wait for the blessed hope—the appearing of the glory of our great God and Saviour, Jesus Christ, who gave himself for us to redeem us from all wickedness.' Titus 2 11-14. There it is again – to rescue us from all wickedness. The wickedness is out there, along with the temptation, the self-willed arrogance, the self-righteous complacency, the without-God-ness, and for all of which there will be a reckoning.

But and there is always a 'but'. Life is full of buts and caveats and conditions. But there are also gospel 'buts'. Here's one from this letter to Titus. 'But when the kindness and love of God our Saviour appeared, he saved us, not because of righteous things we had done, but because of his mercy. He saved us through the washing of rebirth and renewal by the Holy Spirit.' That it might be said is what Christmas is all about. The gospel 'but', without caveats and conditions. Our own restricted Covid-Christmas takes second place when we consider the unrestricted breadth of the gospel invitation: 'For the grace of God has appeared that offers salvation to all people.'

Do you know what the greatest tragedy of this whole Covid disaster is? It is that even when it has given us opportunity repeatedly to reflect on who we are before God, we have failed to do it. We heard the warning about Covid, and even then we have not been even handed in our response to that, but more importantly we have failed to heed the other invitation. For that there will be a reckoning. Let's hear it again: 'For the grace of God has appeared that offers salvation to all people.'

Missing again

He's gone missing again. It wasn't the first time. It wouldn't be the last. In the end they got used to it, or worked it out, but they don't appear to have copied the habit. At least not for now. For certain, after it was all over, in the times ahead, they would have developed the pattern of going missing from time to time. Because they had to.

On this occasion it had been a long day. An ever so long day. They had walked to the church, the synagogue, all together, as one band of brothers. After the service they were all invited to Simon's house. The whole crew. That was a bit awkward. There was upset at the home. The mother-in-law had a fever and was in bed. The wife, I guess, was a bit frantic. Frantic with worry. Frazzled that this noisy bunch of men were crowding into their small home.

Of course Jesus did what Jesus always did. Jesus only did. He sought out where there was grief and met it, among the tears and anxious cries. The narrative in Mark chapter 1 puts it simply, that 'Jesus went to her, took her by the hand and helped her up. The fever left her and she began to wait on them.' That changed the atmosphere in the house and at the lunch party. It seemed, too, to have a knock on effect on the whole day. That act of healing seemed to have triggered a momentum through the whole town. Again as Mark so sparsely writes, 'that evening after sunset the people brought to Jesus all the sick and demon possessed. The whole town gathered at the door, and Jesus healed many who had various diseases.' And by the end of it the disciples were exhausted, and all they had done was fuss around and marshall the crowd. The wife was exhausted as was the mother-in-law. As of course was Jesus.

Somehow they all found a spot to crash out in the house and sleep the sleep of the just. When Simon and the others bleary eyed awoke around sunrise, and chatted the usual first thing trivia, they noticed that he was missing. He was gone. He wasn't in the house. He wasn't in the garden. He wasn't in the street talking with the early tradesman. He was gone. He was nowhere. And soon the crowds were back, asking for Jesus, and the disciples felt like mugs because all they could say was he was missing.

Eventually they tracked him down. Mark again: 'very early in the morning, while it was still dark, Jesus got up, left the house and went off to a solitary place, where he prayed.'

That was when he went missing. To pray. As he said once to his mother, do you not know I should be about my Father's business? This was his Father's business – to pray. Simon himself caught some of this, because years later he wrote: 'humble yourselves under the mighty hand of God and in due time he will lift you up. Cast all your anxiety on him, for he cares for you.' 1 Peter 5.6-7.

There is a point where all this is leading. It is this. We need to go missing. More often.

If Covid would teach us anything it should be this. Apart from follow the science, apart from hands, face and space, if Covid would teach us anything it should be this: that we need to go missing. More often. That we should find that place of prayer. You won't read it in a government pamphlet, though seriously that is part of the problem – we should. We will find it, though, with Christ in his school of prayer.

Covid has given us space. Personal space. We should take it. "Prayer is the soul's sincere desire, uttered, or unexpressed, the motion of a hidden fire that trembles in the breast. Prayer is the Christian's vital breath, the Christian's native air. The upward glancing of an eye when none but God is near." (James Montgomery).

I am talking to myself now. I think I should go missing more often.

The Government Order

In those days an order went out from Westminster, that London and the south east should be placed in Tier 4, and shops should be closed, and transport be limited, and households should not mix, and people should not return to their family home but spend the lockdown in their own household bubble. This was the order that took place when Boris Johnson was Prime Minister of Britain, Matt Hancock was Health Secretary, Sir Patrick Vallance was the Government Chief Scientific Advisor and Professor Chris Whitty was Chief Medical Officer. The order was given as an urgent attempt to stem the spread of a new variant strain of the coronavirus. Other regions of the United Kingdom instituted similar measures. All people found this irksome at this festive season. Many found it distressing. Most people complied with the letter of the order, many with the spirit of the order, some ignored the order, and some just didn't really understand it.

In Luke's gospel this is recorded: 'In those days Caesar Augustus issued a decree that a census should be taken of the entire Roman world. (This was the first census that took place while Quirinius was governor of Syria). And everyone went to his own town to register. So Joseph also went up from the town of Nazareth in Galilee to Judea, to Bethlehem the town of David, because he belonged to the house and line of David. He went there to register with Mary, who was pledged to be married to him and was expecting a child.' Luke 2.1-5.

The Roman authorities issued this order, because some group of bureaucrats thought it a good idea and liked collecting data, or because it was another exercise of imperial control of subject peoples, or because frankly they wanted the money and so they taxed the people.

Most people complied with the letter of the order, many with the spirit of the order, some ignored the order, and some just didn't really understand it. All people found this irksome at this time. Many found it distressing. Doubtless Joseph and Mary had the same bundle of reactions to this imposition. It did not come at a good time for them. And yet they learned that even out of this disruption good would come, and that the purposes of God could become evident. On reflection, looking back years later, I think they never regretted the difficulty of those days, and the extraordinary things they experienced in Bethlehem. Even that itself, going the eighty mile journey by foot, or maybe by donkey for some of the way, was a part of the purposes of God; because in that journey from back country Nazareth to Bethlehem in Judea they stepped into the prophetic pathway of God: 'But you, Bethlehem Ephrathah, though you are small among the clans of Judah, out of you will come for me one who will be ruler over Israel, whose origins are from of old, from days of eternity.' Micah 5.2.

Lord, grant to us to find purpose at this time. Grant to us to know the truth of those famous words: 'We know that in all things God works for the good of those who love him, who have been called according to his purpose.' Romans 8.28.

Grant to us, Lord, to find purpose in restrictions, to find strength in difficulty, to find opportunity in importunity, to find reflection in quietness. Lord, grant us the eyes to see and the ears to hear.

Amen.

The Journey

We were all on a journey. Well, not literally, because we were not really supposed to go anywhere. The ports barely open, and container lorries stacked back up the motorway. The ferries not always running. The airports unlikely to take you anywhere you want, or quarantine you on return. Nevertheless we are all on a journey.

The Wise Men were on a journey, following a star. They clearly had better luck than I did, going out one night to look for the Bethlehem star, thought perhaps to be that glorious and rare conjunction of Saturn and Jupiter, visible for us one December evening in the south western sky after sunset. Only there was nothing for me to see apart from clouds and then driving rain. Good job it was a clear sky for those Magi on the nights they were looking out, otherwise they would have missed the sign, assuming that was the sign, and might have had to wait a few more centuries for another such appearance. That would have rendered their now world famous journey a non starter. Nevertheless we are all on a journey.

Mary and Joseph were on a journey. It was a journey to take, rain or shine. It was a 'have to' journey, which doubtless they took along with others making that enforced trek. Theirs was literally a driving home for Christmas, if you can call walking with or riding the donkey driving. Probably only Mary and Joseph realised it was Christmas, because at some point soon the Christ would be born. But in other ways, theirs too, I guess, was something of a shared journey experience. To quote Chris Rea, "I take a look at the driver next to me. He's just the same. He's driving home, driving home for Christmas." There is something affirmative in knowing that we travel a similar road. And nevertheless we are all on a journey.

It's funny how things turn out. The Magi began on a conscious adventure, 'field and fountain, moor and mountain, following yonder star', that unfolded in ways they just didn't expect, and ended in a dramatic escape, disappearing into unknown history, yet nevertheless taking away with them their life changing story. Mary and Joseph's journey was intentional alright, but they may not have thought it an adventure. Certainly it wouldn't have been the way they planned it, but clearly it was the way God had planned it, and they learned on that journey more of the patience of faith and the at times unseen expectation of hope. It became more true than Mary had imagined when at the beginning of her new direction life journey, she had said, 'I am the Lord's servant. May it be to me as you have said.' (Luke 1.38).

I am afraid that plans changed. Yes, they pretty well changed for everyone at Christmas. What if they are changing more substantially, more significantly? Do we have the wise men's seizing of half an opportunity, or Mary and Joseph's strength of acceptance of change? Both are signs of faith.

Or to put it in the words of songwriters Hall and Maher, "Is there room in your heart for God to write His story? You can come as you are, but it may set you apart when you make room in your heart and trade your dreams for His glory. Make room in your heart."

We could be at a seminal point in our story, in our journey. Will we make room in our heart? Will we make room in our heart for God to write his journey?

Nevertheless we are all on a journey, but is there room in my heart, your heart, for God to write his story?

The Place

It wasn't much of a place. It wasn't much of a place to have a baby. Hopefully he wouldn't come for a few days. Maybe by that time a better place would have been available in town. Life is full of 'maybes'. No different for Mary and Joseph. No different for us.

It wasn't much of a place. It wasn't much of a place to have a baby. Probably they felt that this wasn't how it was meant to be. How could it have meant to be like this. The euphoria of the angel's visit in the comfort of her own home all those months away must have seemed a long time ago. Right now she was probably wanting to be there, back home, with mum around the corner, and aunts ready to help when the baby came. How could this poor lowly stable, with the oxen standing by, be the place where the birth was meant to be! No different for Mary and Joseph. No different for us. Sometimes things don't seem as they are meant to be.

It wasn't much of a place. It wasn't much of a place to have a baby. There didn't seem to be much of a choice. The fact is that there was no room in the inn. No room in the inn. Of all the expectations of coming back to Joseph's home town, I bet he hadn't calculated that, when he told Mary they had to go, because it was a government order. Or if he feared it, he kept his worries to himself, hoping everything would be alright. I think men hope that everything will be alright, blithely muttering with Mr Micawber that 'something will turn up', and it did for Joseph. He found somewhere for his expecting wife to prepare for birth, and it wasn't much of a place. It wasn't much of a place to have a baby. No different for Mary and Joseph. No different for us. Sometimes there doesn't seem to be much of a choice.

Sometimes there doesn't seem to be much of a choice. Sometimes there is the making the best of the situation and trusting that God would make something of it. Sometimes there is the taking of a situation as it is and giving it to God's hands and seeing what He will do with it. For Mary and Joseph when they did that, God came. God came and Christ was born. O holy night! And the holiness lay in trusting God in what was not much of a place. Not much of a place to have a baby. Not much of a place to bear the Christ child. Or perhaps it was and there was never such a right place for grace to appear, for the grace of God to be shown in its true transparent glory, unfettered by stuff, uncluttered by protocol and preparation. It wasn't much of a place, but it was the right place, God's place.

It wasn't much of a place. Sometimes things don't seem as they are meant to be. Sometimes there doesn't seem to be much of a choice. Sometimes there is the making the best of the situation and trusting that God would make something of it. Sometimes there is the taking of a situation as it is and giving it to God's hands and seeing what He will do with it. Lord, make it so for us this Covid-Christmas, for this Covid-New Year, for this Covid-future. For this out of Lockdown future. For this new normal future.

Here is faith. Here is God at work: 'While they were there, the time came for the baby to be born and she gave birth to her firstborn, a son. She wrapped him in cloths and place him in a manger, for there was no room for them in the inn.' Luke 2.6-7. Not much of a place. It was the right place. Thank God.

Lockdown Blues

Damned if they do. Damned if they don't. Who'd be a government leader?

A bubble of one, a bubble of two, a bubble burst. I'm forever blowing bubbles, pretty bubbles in the air.

Afraid to be. Unafraid to be. Unable to decide. Quick to decide.

Irked by restrictions, comfortable with restrictions. Compliant with the guidelines, defiant of the guidelines. Complicit with the instructions, navigating the instructions.

Working with, working through, working against them.

Driving home for Christmas, staying home for Christmas.

Vacation, staycation, lost my passport anyway.

Quarantined, vaccined, caffeine and benzene.

Adrenaline, baked bean, staff canteen. It's closed.

Online shop delivery, Covid-19 recovery, vaccine discovery, politicians jittery.

Winter misery, Christmas mystery, post lockdown liberty, but real liberty is internally.

Inside, not on the outside.

Choices narrow, choices wide. Attitudes humble or full of pride.

Ebb and flow of life, turning of the tide. Always waiting for the tide.

If only it was so simple.

It's coming nearer, it's getting further. He's had it, she's got it, they don't believe it.

They've conspired but he's expired and few seem inspired. Possibly politicians mired.

"Rage, rage against the dying of the light. Do not go gentle into that good night."

'The people walking in darkness have seen a great light. On those living in the land of the shadow of death a great light has shined.'

I don't want some mirage in the desert. I never have.

I don't want a pot of gold at the foot of the rainbow. I never have.

I don't want a scratch card to take my money, give me some back, and take it back again. I never have.

I don't want some false hope, false dream, some half-truth. No equivocation.

Perhaps the whole truth and nothing but the truth, so help me God.

I want God's truth. Straight up, plain and simple, I want God's Truth.

The Truth that levels up and levels down, that makes the last first and the first last.

The Truth that tells it straight how I am. That tells me of mercy and grace.

No questions, just the answers.

I want this. I want Christ. This is an Advent message. This is a New Year message.

This is all I want for Christmas.

This is what I want in lockdown and out of lockdown.

I want it in Tier One and Tier Two. I want it in Tier Three and Four.

I want it when the pubs are closed and when they are open.

I want it when the churches are closed and when they are open.

'For unto us a child is born, unto us a son is given. And the government will be on his shoulders.'

That's what I want the government on his shoulders.

His government in my life on his shoulders.

That's the great light I want to see. That's the dawning I want to wake for.

That's what I want.

What do you want?

Robert Musgrave

End Words

When Noah and his family came out of Lockdown, after weeks and weeks of confinement, not really knowing what was going on in the outside world, what would be the same, what would be different, they saw a rainbow and they took it for a sign. They took it for a sign that some things would be different, and that some things could be relied upon. Always. They took it for a sign of hope. From then on, they always took it as a sign of hope.

In the middle of summer 2020 there was a beautiful rainbow arcing its colours over Clapham Common and south London. We saw it too in Battersea. A friend sent me a picture the same day of a rainbow in Devon, and another of one in Sussex by the sea. We all took it for a sign of hope.

The apostle Paul wrote 'that suffering produces perseverance, perseverance character, and character hope, and hope does not disappoint us, because God has poured out his love into our hearts by the Holy Spirit.' (Romans 5.5)

As I write this there is much hope as well as much weariness, as in all the seasons of life. We are being vaccinated and refusing to be vaccinated. We are making plans for restaurants to re-open and for businesses to close. We are planning vacations but some are content with staycations. We are still burying loved ones and welcoming loved ones back. Whatever we do, we do not stand still.

I will continue to write Words for each Day. I will continue to watch and to reflect. I will continue to hope.

Robert Musgrave.

Words in a Lockdown Year

by Robert George Musgrave MBE.

If you have enjoyed reading this book, you might also enjoy other short books by Robert Musgrave:

'Looking Backwards, Going Forwards' – *Thinking aloud with Psalms 150-139.*

'Chasing after the Wind – *100 Days with Ecclesiastes.*

To read more about the work of Providence House, you might like to read:

'The Young Woman Who Lived in a Shoe' by Elizabeth Braund MBE.

All available from Providence House, 138 Falcon Road, London SW11 2LW.
www.providence-house.org

All profits from this book go to The Providence House Trust.
Charity number: 1181473.

Printed in Great Britain
by Amazon